D1296202

COST-BENEFIT
ANALYSIS

To Paula

COST-BENEFIT ANALYSIS
Theory and Application

TEVFIK F. NAS

SAGE Publications
International Educational and Professional Publisher
Thousand Oaks London New Delhi

Copyright © 1996 by Sage Publications, Inc.

All rights reserved. No part of this book may be reproduced or utilized in any form or by any means, electronic or mechanical, including photocopying, recording, or by any information storage and retrieval system, without permission in writing from the publisher.

For information address:

 SAGE Publications, Inc.
2455 Teller Road
Thousand Oaks, California 91320
E-mail: order@sagepub.com

SAGE Publications Ltd.
6 Bonhill Street
London EC2A 4PU
United Kingdom

SAGE Publications India Pvt. Ltd.
M-32 Market
Greater Kailash I
New Delhi 110 048 India

Printed in the United States of America

Library of Congress Cataloging-in-Publication Data

Nas, Tevfik F.
    Cost-benefit analysis: Theory and application / author, Tevfik F. Nas.
        p.   cm.
    Includes bibliographical references and index.
    ISBN 0-8039-7132-X (acid-free paper).—ISBN 0-8039-7133-8 (pbk.: acid-free paper)
        1. Cost effectiveness.   2. Welfare economics.   3. Finance, Public.
    4. Economic development projects—Cost effectiveness.   I. Title.
    HB846.2.N37   1996
    658.15'54—dc20   95-41788

This book is printed on acid-free paper.

96   97   98   99   10   9   8   7   6   5   4   3   2   1

Sage Production Editor: Diane S. Foster
Sage Typesetter: Andrea D. Swanson

Contents

Figures

Preface

This book is written for students who are enrolled in a one-term course in cost-benefit analysis (CBA) as part of a public finance sequence. It is designed to serve as a textbook for undergraduate students in economics, public administration, and public policy studies. Additionally, it has features that would make it accessible as a primary text for the master of public administration and master of public policy programs and a valuable source for courses on environment, natural resources, urban studies, and health care.

A typical economics student taking a CBA course will have satisfied the minimum requirements of the economics curriculum, including principles of microeconomics. However, students from other disciplines sometimes lack the necessary preparation in economics, thereby making text assignment quite difficult for instructors who are practitioners or professors specialized in the field of public finance. To fill this gap, this book is written in a style and detail that could be easily used by students who have little preparation in economics.

The book includes recent developments in the theoretical and empirical CBA literature. It is composed of three parts, each with unique features that would be of interest to a wide audience. The first part (Chapters 1-3) covers the standard topic of public finance. To lead students into the thought process of CBA, this part provides a detailed discussion of welfare economics and microeconomic foundations of

CBA. Although students with a strong background in economics might find the material useful as a refresher, they may choose to skip this section. The second part (Chapters 4-10) is devoted to the fundamentals of CBA. Rather than a condensed discussion of the CBA methodology limited to only one chapter, such as that found in most public finance books, this part provides a comprehensive analysis. There are seven chapters, each with a thorough treatment of the stages of public policy analysis combined with examples that clarify theoretical issues on identification, measurement, and comparison of costs and benefits. The third part (Chapters 11-14) examines the current state of the art in CBA as practiced by public and international agencies and deals with some of the application issues in the areas of health care and the environment.

Early versions of this work were used as teaching material in the MPA program at the University of Michigan, Flint. Over the years, it has evolved into its present form through various revisions in response to the needs of enthusiastic students and developments in the literature. The content has benefited greatly from the analytical details of three classics in the field: E. J. Mishan's *Cost-Benefit Analysis*, E. M. Gramlich's *A Guide to Benefit-Cost Analysis*, and R. W. Tresch's *Public Finance: A Normative Theory*; it also integrated new approaches and ideas from a growing body of literature on applications. The final draft of the book reflects valuable contributions from reviewers, colleagues, and students. I wish to thank Peter Carayannopoulos, John P. Forrester, Dipak K. Gupta, Wade E. Martin, Gary Mattson, Dale Matcheck, Albert Price, and Mehmet Odekon, who provided useful feedback, ideas, and helpful comments, and William Desvousges for providing valuable applied materials. Several individuals at the EPA, GAO, CBO, and the World Bank provided information that helped me structure the applied section of the book; and my appreciation is in order for Judy Bedore, Joseph Dorris, Bonnie Kincaid, Ginny Lagather, and Michael Wickerham for their encouragement and assistance. I am grateful to the staff at Sage Publications, especially to Renee Piernot, Andy Swanson, Gillian Dickens, and Diane Foster. Also, a special thanks goes to my wife Paula, who supported me at every development stage of this project both as an editor, an ardent critique, and as a colleague with excellent ideas and insight that pretty much set the tone of the book. Finally, how can I forget our little daughter Megan, who reminded us of the true meaning of costs and benefits, especially when playtime was at issue.

1

Introduction

This book is about making decisions. Rather than looking at decisions in general, it focuses on those that relate to the well-being of a community, a region, or society at large. On a regular basis, individuals in the public domain confront issues that have important ramifications for the welfare of current and future generations. Should a city council appropriate additional funds to increase the size of the police force, or should it encourage the formation of citizen watch groups instead? What are the costs and benefits of developing and implementing national guidelines for securing minimum water quality standards? Is further downsizing of national defense feasible? What would be the net benefits of introducing the nation's high schools to the challenges of today's interactive digital communication systems? In these and similar examples, common sense and intuition quite often steer decision makers in the right direction. However, to ensure efficiency in resource allocation and to achieve maximum gains in social welfare, it may be necessary to use evaluation procedures that are based on systematic and careful assessment of all options under consideration.

One such procedure is cost-benefit analysis (CBA), a method distinctively developed for the evaluation of public policy issues. Under the CBA methodology, all potential gains and losses from a proposal

1

are identified, converted into monetary units, and compared on the basis of decision rules to determine if the proposal is desirable from society's standpoint. When considering the feasibility of cleaning contaminated water wells in a region, for example, the analyst needs to consider all related costs and benefits, including those that are indirect and intangible. A comprehensive evaluation of this type of project will take into account the potential effect on both human lives and the environment. Also considered in the evaluation will be the impact on future generations and the welfare of different socioeconomic groups. Once all relevant information has been gathered, properly quantified, and compared using such methods as net present value, internal rate of return, and/or benefit-cost ratios, the analyst decides whether the proposal is beneficial from society's point of view.

As we show in this book, CBA is a highly detailed and comprehensive procedure. Its method and analytical details differ from those of other project evaluation tools, in particular from financial analysis.[1] Financial analysis is used primarily in the private sector to determine which outcomes are best from the perspective of private interests. The streams of expected cash and revenues are considered as benefits, and direct payments to factors of production are viewed as costs regardless of their output effects elsewhere in the economy. Costs to third-party individuals, such as environmental damage for which the private entity has no obligation to pay, are excluded from the cost-revenue calculations.

CBA, on the other hand, is particularly designed for the evaluation of public projects, and the project outcome is always evaluated on the basis of public interest. Unlike financial analysis, where all relevant cost and benefit items are measured in observed market prices, valuation in CBA is made by prices corrected for possible market distortions. It is important to note that costs and benefits are measured in terms of social utility gains and losses rather than cash or revenue flows, and external costs and benefits are invariably included in the evaluation.

CBA also differs from cost-effectiveness analysis (CEA), a method that ranks outcomes that cannot be measured or compared to costs in dollar terms. A major difference between these two methods relates to the measure of benefit outcome: In CEA, it is expressed in non-monetary units, such as the number of lives saved, whereas in CBA, it is measured in dollar terms. There are other differences in terms of analytical detail, but as discussed in Chapter 4, the methods are essentially similar, and both are frequently used to assess the economic and social impact of projects.

THEORETICAL FOUNDATIONS AND THE RATIONALE FOR CBA

Public project analysis requires a general framework within which costs and benefits can be identified and assessed from society's perspective.[2] Welfare economics and public finance provide the theoretical foundations for such a framework. Both fields justify government involvement in the economy, examine the extent of government's influence on the private sector, and analyze the nature of its impact on the welfare level of society at large.

Government intervenes in the private economy in response to market failure, such as imperfect competition, a lack of information, an inability to provide public goods, or the presence of externalities, all of which impede the market's progress toward complying with society's allocation and distribution norms. As a provider, government raises funds through taxation or borrowing and uses these funds to provide a variety of public goods and services. As a regulator, it intervenes when the market is burdened by negative externalities, such as excessive pollution or hazardous waste, in which case government regulates by setting standards, clarifying property rights, or imposing prohibitive taxes to curtail the sources of such activities.[3] It also steps in by legislating antitrust laws and price regulations when the private market is dominated by one or a few firms that constrain the workings of the market mechanism.

Another role of government is to maintain income distribution along the lines of society's welfare norms.[4] Income distribution attained through the private market may diverge from its socially desired level and place those income groups that lack resources at a disadvantage in generating an adequate income. To narrow the distribution gap among income groups, government implements corrective devices: It levies progressive taxes, and it redistributes income by using various forms of federal grants or welfare programs.

Each of these public sector interventions has a profound impact on society's resource base. Because the price mechanism is nonfunctional in these areas of market failure, public policy makers face the task of uncovering society's preferences for, and the costs of, such allocations. Cost-benefit analysis is one method commonly used to analyze and evaluate public policies. Not only is it a framework that draws on the fundamental principles of welfare economics and public finance, but it is also a way of thinking, because it provides guidance for public policy makers in their search for a resource allocation that would be best suited to society's efficiency and equity objectives.

THE APPLICATION OF CBA: A BRIEF HISTORY

The CBA methodology has evolved over the years with increased acceptance by numerous disciplines and government agencies.[5] Formally, it became part of the Flood Control Act of 1936, and with a landmark 1950 report prepared by the Federal Interagency River Basin Committee, it evolved into a standard guide for water resources planners. The most systematic use of the method occurred in the 1960s, when the Planning, Programming and Budgeting System (PPBS) was introduced as an extension of system analysis in the Department of Defense.

After the 1960s, the impact of CBA on the design and formulation of policies in federal agencies increased significantly. Through the guidance of the Office of Management and Budget (OMB), CBA has become an essential evaluation tool, incorporating straightforward guidelines consistent with the premises and the logic of CBA.

OMB has since been instrumental in integrating the principles of CBA in the decision-making process in federal agencies. Periodically, OMB sends circulars to the heads of executive departments and agencies providing guidance on the use of CBA in evaluating federal programs. Circular A-94 (U.S. Office of Management and Budget 1992), for example, clearly states the purpose of its guidelines to be the promotion of "efficient resource allocation through well-informed decision making by the Federal Government." It specifically stresses the point that the guidelines must be followed in "all analyses submitted to OMB in support of legislative and budget programs."

Below, we highlight some of the important rules included in the Circular.[6]

1. Estimates of expected costs and benefits must be provided and defined from the perspective of society rather than the Federal Government.
2. Both intangible and tangible benefits and costs should be included in the analysis.
3. Costs should be defined in terms of opportunity cost, and incremental costs and benefits rather than sunk costs should be used in the benefit-cost computations.
4. Real economic values rather than transfer payments should be included in the net benefit calculation. Transfer payments may be considered and discussed in terms of distributional aspects.
5. In measuring the costs and benefits, the concept of consumer surplus must be employed, and whenever applicable willingness to pay must be estimated directly and indirectly.
6. Market prices provide an "invaluable starting point" for measurement, but in the presence of market failures and price distortions, shadow prices may have to be employed.
7. The decision whether to accept a public project must be based on the standard criterion of net present value. To furnish additional information on the project, the internal rate of return also can be provided.
8. In reporting net present value and other criteria, a real discount rate of seven percent (the average pretax rate of return on average private investment in recent years) should be used. Also, a sensitivity analysis with alternative discount rates should be provided.

This checklist, which summarizes the most essential steps outlined in the Circular, is quite in line with the underlying economic theory and the principles of CBA. Noteworthy is the parallel between this checklist and the rules to be followed in identifying, classifying, and measuring costs and benefits, as outlined in any CBA text.

THE PLAN OF THE BOOK

From the preceding, it is clear that the CBA methodology encompasses a great deal more than simple cost-benefit calculations. The analyst must painstakingly identify all relevant costs and benefits and measure their true resource values under alternative policy and economic environments. CBA is an art, and to conduct a reliable evaluation, the analyst needs to be equipped with all necessary analytical tools and economic concepts that will lead to that end.

Throughout the text, we rely on economic theory as we develop the principles of CBA. The following two chapters provide a fairly comprehensive coverage of the relevant topics of microeconomics, public finance, and welfare economics. Chapter 2 describes the criteria by which we judge the private market's performance in resource allocation and income distribution. It concentrates on the efficiency criterion known as Pareto optimality and describes a resource allocation that is both efficient and fair according to society's distributional norms. Chapter 3 reexamines the efficiency concept in the public sector. A brief discussion of market failures is followed by statements of Pareto and potential Pareto optimality conditions in the presence of imperfectly competitive markets, public goods, and externalities. The chapter also discusses some of the collective decision-making rules as a first step in the analysis of public sector expenditures.

The next seven chapters are devoted to the fundamentals of CBA. Chapter 4 is an overview of the CBA methodology; it outlines the main steps involved in the evaluation of a project. Chapter 5 provides an analytical framework for formulating, identifying, and evaluating all possible allocational outcomes in project evaluation. It introduces the concept of consumer surplus, discusses alternative measures of welfare change, and explains how these measures are used to identify the costs and benefits of a project.

Chapter 6 deals with the quantification of costs and benefits when market prices do exist. The first- and second-best orthodoxies, which form the logical basis for choosing either market or adjusted prices as efficiency measures, are introduced and applied to make the necessary adjustments when the sources of price distortions are known. Chapter 7 addresses the valuation question in cases where price information may be limited or unobtainable in an existing market. The focus of the chapter is nonmarket valuation techniques, such as the contingent valuation method. A brief review of several direct and indirect approaches to the valuation of nonmarketed goods is followed by a case study highlighting the application of the contingent valuation method to a specific valuation problem of an environmental good. The chapter also looks at some of the arguments and controversies surrounding the issue of how to measure the value of time and human life as two specific intangibles.

Chapters 8 and 9 describe the procedure for discounting the future stream of costs and benefits, analyze different perspectives on what constitutes a theoretically acceptable discount rate, and provide an overview of investment decision rules. Chapter 10 deals with distributional aspects of public expenditure analysis and illustrates several approaches that may be used to incorporate both allocational and distributional considerations in project evaluation.

The final four chapters are devoted to the discussion of real-world applications of CBA. Chapter 11 begins with a summary of the major conclusions of the preceding chapters. It provides a list of rules to follow when identifying and valuing costs and benefits, describes an evaluation design for a typical analysis, and outlines the EPA guidelines for the evaluation of regulatory options as one example of CBA applications. Chapters 12 and 13 cover issues of evaluation in the areas of health care and the environment. Finally, Chapter 14 examines the current state of the art in CBA as practiced by international agencies.

SUMMARY

This chapter outlined the main features of the market system and highlighted the major areas of government involvement in the private market. The dynamics and failures of the market system were briefly described and used in support of the arguments for the traditional role of government in a private market setting.

Having justified the use of CBA in the public sector, the chapter previewed the most unique features of CBA. These are (a) costs and benefits of a public project are identified and valued from society's perspective; (b) both costs and benefits are quantified and expressed in monetary units; (c) the future stream of benefits and costs is discounted to a single time dimension by a socially relevant discount rate; and (d) project selection is based on the fundamental principle of maximizing social net benefits.

Drawing on the theory of welfare economics and public finance, the chapter compared CBA to other decision-making frameworks, with particular emphasis on financial analysis. In financial analysis, the returns to a project are measured in terms of revenue or cash flows, and the feasibility of a project is viewed and evaluated from the perspective of private entities. Unlike financial analysis, costs and benefits in CBA are measured in terms of welfare losses and gains rather than cash or revenue flows. Another important difference is that CBA considers costs and benefits to third parties as long as they involve real resource use and produce output gains. Financial analysis will exclude such third-party effects if they involve no obligation to make a payment or receive compensation.

The chapter also provided an overview of the theory and application of CBA. A brief history of CBA preceded a summary outline of what lies ahead.

NOTES

1. For a comparison of CBA with other frameworks, see Smith (1986).

2. Within this theoretical context, CBA accounts for all of the allocational and distributional effects of government projects. For example, cleaning up the environment or improving social infrastructure always leads to resource reallocation and some welfare changes among members of society. From such public policy measures, some may gain at the expense of others, few may lose despite the corrective measures taken by the government, or, as is often the case, potential gains may be lost because of the distortionary effects of government involvement. Therefore, it is important that any public project is evaluated in a context where efficiency and equity aspects of government involvement in the private economy are defined and analyzed from society's point of view.

3. When positive externalities are present, government encourages production. In the case of education, for example, it introduces educational subsidies or tax preferences to encourage enrollment in educational institutions, thus providing schooling to larger segments of society.

4. Government also performs a stabilization function that is beyond the scope of this book. Stabilization policies, such as monetary and fiscal policies, are used by government when an economy experiences cyclical variations of aggregate demand and output. To moderate the adverse effects of inflation and unemployment problems, government may introduce countercyclical discretionary policies. For a review of government's three functions, see Musgrave and Musgrave (1989, chap. 1).

5. This section draws on the work of Nelson (1987). See Campen (1986, chap. 2) for more on the history of CBA.

6. The CBA guidelines in Circular A-94 are to be followed for the analysis of public investments and regulations. Water resource projects, acquisition of commercial-type services, and federal energy programs were exempted from the Circular.

DISCUSSION QUESTIONS

1. In which specific areas does government intervene in the private economy? What is the economic rationale underlying its involvement?
2. What is the role of government in a market economy? Which of the main functions that government serves are appropriate for cost-benefit analysis?
3. What are the main differences between financial analysis and cost-benefit analysis?
4. Explain how cost-effectiveness analysis differs from cost-benefit analysis.

2

Economic Efficiency, Income Distribution, and the Market Mechanism

This chapter establishes the theoretical foundation for the analysis of public projects and describes the efficiency rules for making cost-benefit decisions. To that end, it reviews the main features of the competitive market system and the conditions under which efficiency in resource allocation is attained. The first section focuses on the efficiency criterion known as Pareto optimality and provides a detailed discussion of the conditions that must be met to achieve a Pareto-optimal allocation. The second section begins with a brief depiction of society's welfare function and accordingly defines a resource allocation that is both efficient and equitable. The final section illustrates how market forces work toward achieving a Pareto-optimal solution and looks at situations where the market fails to do so.

EFFICIENCY NORM: PARETO OPTIMALITY

Resource allocation decisions in a free market economy are based on information generated by the price mechanism. As prices vary, producers adjust output, supplying the market with a quantity of output that maximizes profit (or minimizes losses). If, as a result of price variations, a particular industry becomes more profitable, then the established firms of that industry increase their output. Also, new firms enter the industry and divert resources from other, less productive uses, thereby improving social welfare. If an industry incurs economic losses, on the other hand, firms with temporary losses contract output, and those with longer term losses leave the industry in search of more profitable prospects. This process continues until the market reaches a level of allocation where no further improvement in social welfare is possible. Such an allocational outcome is known as *Pareto optimum.*

Pareto optimality, named after the Italian economist Vilfredo Pareto (1848-1923), is an efficiency norm describing the conditions necessary to achieve optimality in resource allocation. It is *a state of economic affairs where no one can be made better off without simultaneously making at least one other person worse off.* For example, if a resource allocation is such that no additional investment in information infrastructure is possible without reducing investment in other areas, such as defense, education, or health care, then Pareto efficiency has been attained. In this situation, no further gain in welfare is possible because no one can be made better off without at the same time making someone worse off.

Note that Pareto efficiency defined as such is limited: It only applies to reallocation decisions that improve society's well-being if at least one individual is made better off and no one is made worse off. In most real-world situations, however, welfare improves at the expense of at least one person becoming worse off; therefore, gains in welfare can be viewed as potential rather than actual Pareto improvement. As discussed later in the chapter, those individuals who benefit from a reallocation must be able to compensate those individuals who lose. When that is the case, a resource reallocation that raises net social benefits can be judged by the potential Pareto condition.

In what follows, graphical depictions are provided of both Pareto and potential Pareto optimality, and the three underlying efficiency conditions are described. These are production efficiency, exchange efficiency, and allocative efficiency.[1]

Production Efficiency

Production efficiency represents a resource allocation where it is no longer possible to increase the output of one good without reducing the output of some other good. Referring to the previous example, it is that allocation where improved information infrastructure can be built only by reducing production in other areas. Sometimes, resource allocation could be such that an improvement in one area requires no cutback in others. While maintaining the existing level of military appropriations, for example, it may be possible to develop a more sophisticated information infrastructure with a given resource base. When this is the case, the existing allocation is Pareto inefficient, and any policy that would improve information technology without reducing output levels in other sectors of the economy will be viewed as a Pareto improvement.

Such allocations representing production efficiency are illustrated by the *production possibilities curve PP* in Figure 2.1. The curve *PP* illustrates the maximum attainable amounts of two goods (X and Y) that could be produced with a given resource base and technology. Points on the frontier, such as *a* and *b*, represent Pareto efficiency. Those below the frontier, such as *c*, represent inefficient use of resources. Through a movement from *c* to either *a* or *b*, output can be raised in one sector without reducing output in the other. For example, as the output combination changes from *c* to *b*, the production of X increases with no corresponding change in the production of Y. From *c* to *a*, the production of Y increases with no decline in the production of X. Once the frontier has been reached, additional factor movements will result in increased output in one sector at the expense of the other.

A movement from *a* to *b* will cause factor utilization levels to be altered in both X and Y, resulting in an increase in the quantity of X and a decrease in the quantity of Y produced. The rate at which Y is converted into X is called the *marginal rate of transformation* of Y into X (MRT_{XY}). This rate varies as factors are transferred from *a* to *b*: it is lower at point *a* and rises as resources flow from Y to X along the curve. This means that as the output combination changes from *a* to *b*, society gives up *ac* amount of good Y and gains *cb* amount of good X. Another way of stating this relationship is that MRT is the slope of the *PP* curve and becomes steeper as the output of X rises at the frontier. The steeper the slope, the more costly it is to produce an additional unit of X.

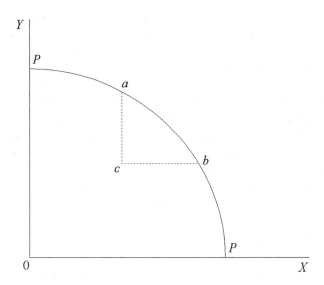

Figure 2.1. Production possibilities frontier.

Note. A move from point *c*, which represents inefficient use of resources, to either *a* or *b* raises output in one sector without reducing output in the other. Points *a* and *b* represent Pareto efficiency. A movement from *a* to *b* results in increased output of *X* and reduced output of *Y*.

Exchange Efficiency

Achieving optimality in resource allocation also requires the presence of exchange efficiency. This simply implies that for a particular allocation to be Pareto optimal, an efficiently produced output combination also must be allocated efficiently among the consumers.

Exchange efficiency is attained when it is impossible to make one individual better off without making one other individual worse off. Returning to the two-individual (*A* and *B*) and two-good (*X* and *Y*) model, both *A* and *B* are assumed to have a utility function representing consumption preferences for alternative combinations of *X* and *Y*. An important property of the utility function is the diminishing nature of the rate of substitution between *X* and *Y*. To have more of *X*, the individual must have less of *Y* to maintain the same utility level.[2]

The rate at which *X* is substituted for *Y* is called the *marginal rate of substitution* of *X* for *Y* (MRS_{XY}). This rate measures the individual's willingness to substitute X for Y at a given level of satisfaction. It changes as more of one good is exchanged for less of the other. For each additional X, for example, the individual will be willing to give up fewer units of Y to remain at the same level of utility.

Note that when A's MRS_{XY} differs from B's MRS_{XY}, any reallocation of X and Y between the two individuals will increase the welfare of one or both individuals without making anyone worse off. Eventually, an efficient allocation corresponding to a particular output combination will be reached when A's MRS_{XY} equals B's MRS_{XY}. At this allocation, it is no longer possible to make either A or B better off without making the other worse off.[3] When such an allocation is reached, efficiency in exchange has been attained.

Allocative Efficiency

To satisfy the allocative efficiency condition, both the exchange and the production efficiency conditions must be met. This means that the rate at which goods are produced (which we defined as MRT) must be equal to the rate at which consumers are willing to substitute one with the other (MRS). Note that every point on the production possibilities curve corresponds to a different set of allocations between the two individuals that satisfies the exchange efficiency condition. When all such points on the production frontier are considered, the number of efficient allocation possibilities becomes infinitely large. Because an efficiently produced bundle of goods (a point from the production frontier with a given MRT) can be allocated between A and B at varying rates, there is at least one particular allocation where

$$MRT_{XY} = MRS_{XY}. \qquad (2.1)$$

This is the allocation that meets both exchange and production efficiency conditions simultaneously.

When such an allocation is attained, the rate at which commodities are substituted in production equals the rate at which they are exchanged in consumption. For example, if MRT_{XY} equals MRS_{XY} at 3/2, then two units of X can be produced only by giving up three units

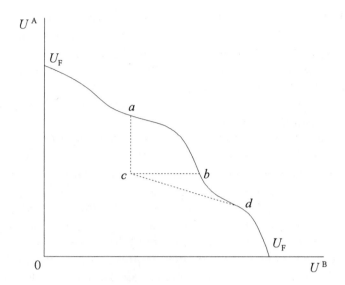

Figure 2.2. Grand utility frontier.

Note. A movement from point *a* to *b* represents an improvement in *B*'s well-being only at the expense of reducing *A*'s well-being. Any point below the frontier represents inefficiency, but any reallocation within the *acb* triangle will increase the welfare of one or both without making anyone worse off. A movement from *c* to *d* is a potential Pareto improvement.

of *Y,* and both *A* and *B* are willing to accept two units of *X* and give up three units of *Y.*

Such allocations are illustrated by the grand utility frontier ($U_F U_F$) in Figure 2.2. The *grand utility frontier* is derived from the production possibilities curve by drawing allocation possibilities for each efficient output combination and specifying only the allocation points where MRT equals MRS.[4] Depicting only those points that are efficient both in production and in exchange, the frontier represents all of the efficient combinations of well-being between *A* and *B*. As shown in the figure, a movement from *a* to *b*, representing an improved well-being for *B*, is only possible at the expense of reduced well-being for *A*. In other words, a rearrangement of resources changing the combination of both goods will not benefit *B* without reducing *A*'s well-being. This is what is implied by a Pareto-optimal allocation.

Note that points below the grand utility frontier are inefficient because it is still possible to improve welfare by reorienting resources to the allocation levels on the frontier. The welfare position represented by point c, for example, can be improved by moving to a, b, or any other position within the ab range. Any reallocation within the acb triangle will increase the welfare of one or both individuals without making anyone worse off.

Also note that a resource reallocation from c to d does not meet Pareto criteria because B becomes better off at A's expense. Such a move is defined as a *potential Pareto improvement* in the sense that d is superior to c, and a movement to d could be made possible by having B compensate A for the loss that results from the reallocation. This move is also called a Kaldor-Hicks improvement, named after British economists Nicholas Kaldor and John Hicks. As discussed in the following chapters, Kaldor-Hicks improvement is commonly used as an efficiency norm in cost-benefit analysis. For example, a public project driving welfare distribution from c to d in Figure 2.2 is considered efficient despite its negative impact on A's welfare. According to this norm, a project that yields positive net benefits is viewed as being acceptable if B could compensate A and still be ahead. However, it is important to note that the compensation need not be carried out.[5]

PARETO OPTIMALITY
AND SOCIAL WELFARE FUNCTION

The preceding discussion clearly shows that by using Pareto optimality as a criterion, it is possible to distinguish between efficient and inefficient utility distributions and to rank those distributions located on the grand utility frontier as superior to those located inside the frontier. What Pareto analysis does not provide is a conceptual framework for comparing two solutions that are efficient. Such comparisons involve ethical judgments and require a formulation of society's distributional norms.

Figure 2.3 depicts a social welfare function that reflects society's distributional ethics. Social indifference curves W_1, W_2, . . . W_n represent alternative combinations of individual utilities among which

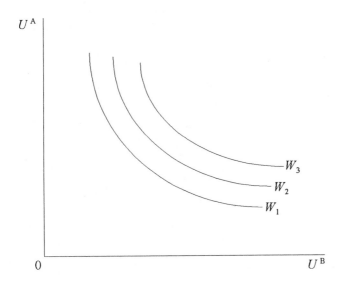

Figure 2.3. Social indifference curves.

Note. Each curve represents alternative combinations of individual utilities among which society is indifferent. Movements along a curve yield no change in welfare, but movements outward from the origin represent improved social welfare.

society is indifferent. A movement along any of these curves represents no change in social welfare: As the utility of one individual increases, the other individuals' utilities must decline if society is to maintain a constant level of welfare. Social welfare improves only when the movement is to a curve farther from the origin: W_2 represents a higher level of welfare than W_1, and W_3 is higher than both W_2 and W_1.

These curves are superimposed on the grand utility frontier in Figure 2.4. Point A, the point of tangency between the frontier and the highest attainable social indifference curve, depicts a situation where society could achieve a *Pareto optimum-welfare maximum* allocation. This point is superior to any other point on the frontier: It is both efficient and equitable from society's perspective.

It should be noted that the Pareto optimum-welfare maximum allocation is attainable at various levels of welfare depending on the type of specification used in assigning distributional weights. The

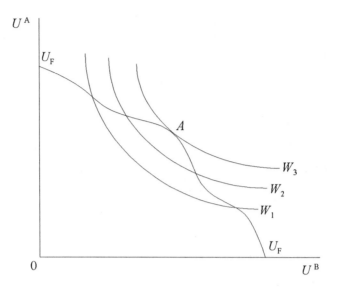

Figure 2.4. Pareto optimum-welfare maximum allocation.

Note. Point *A*, the tangency between the grand utility frontier and the highest attainable social indifference curve, represents a Pareto optimum-welfare maximum allocation. This allocation is both efficient and equitable from society's perspective.

functional form used in Figure 2.4, for example, satisfies the Pareto-optimum criterion; that is, if one individual's utility increases while all other utilities are held constant, social welfare must increase.[6] There are several other formulations that are widely used in economic analyses involving distributional issues. Two of these forms, utilitarianism and Rawlsian distributive justice, are discussed in Chapter 10.

MARKET-DETERMINED ALLOCATION AND EFFICIENCY

The fundamental theorem of welfare economics states that the market mechanism operating in a perfectly competitive environment produces Pareto-optimal solutions. A perfectly competitive market is characterized by the following four conditions:

1. With freely available perfect information about a market transaction, consumers, resource owners, and firms maximize; that is, they choose the outcome yielding the greatest possible net benefits to themselves.
2. Firms are too small in relation to the entire market to influence the market price. Each firm is a price taker: It offers a homogeneous product to many buyers at the market price. Price fixing, price leadership, and monopolistic practices constraining output levels are ruled out by assumption.
3. There are no barriers or structural impediments to prevent firms from entering into or exiting from an industry. Resources are completely mobile, and firms are able to enter freely if an industry is profitable or to leave if losses are expected.
4. All factors of production are privately owned.

Assuming that these conditions are satisfied, the market mechanism generates a set of prices through the interaction of supply and demand. On the demand side of the market, consumers choose consumption levels where the benefit they receive from an additional unit of a product (marginal benefit) equals the price that exists in the market. On the supply side, efficient output is attained at the level where the cost of producing an additional unit (marginal cost) equals the market price. Thus, from both the demand side and the supply side of the market, we obtain an efficient solution where market price equals both marginal benefit (MB) and marginal cost (MC).

As shown in Figure 2.5, the downward sloping line D represents the demand function, indicating the quantities that individuals are willing to buy at alternative prices. Price is inversely related to quantity; the lower the price, the greater the quantity demanded. As the price level decreases, consumers maximize by consuming additional quantities to the point where price equals MB. Hence, at every point on the demand curve, individuals maximize by choosing consumption levels where the benefit they receive from the last unit of output they purchase is the same as the price they pay.

The upward sloping line S is the supply line, indicating the quantities of the good that producers supply to the market at alternative prices. The relationship between price and quantity is direct: Higher quantities are supplied at higher MC, and that requires higher prices to make the additional production feasible for the producers. As the price level rises, producers maximize by supplying additional output to the point where price equals MC.

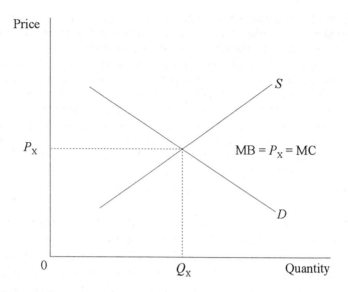

Figure 2.5. Equilibrium in a one-good model.

Note. Equilibrium is attained where marginal benefit equals the price of the good, which equals marginal cost. The point of intersection of the demand curve and the supply curve is the Pareto-optimal solution.

As shown in Figure 2.5, a clearing price (P_X) is obtained where MB equals MC. At this equilibrium price, markets provide an output level Q_X where the cost of producing the last unit equals consumers' marginal valuation of that unit. This equilibrium corresponds to the Pareto-optimal solution described in the preceding section. Any other price-output combination is inefficient, and a move toward the equilibrium price-output level will be considered a Pareto improvement. For example, at output levels below Q_X, the benefit expected from an additional unit of output exceeds the cost of producing that unit. Therefore, producing additional quantities will be a Pareto improvement because each additional unit produced will add more to total benefit than it will to total cost. Additional production will take place until the clearing price is attained. Any price-quantity combination beyond equilibrium is inefficient because marginal cost will exceed marginal benefit, thus adding more to costs than to benefits.

It should be emphasized that market equilibrium produces an efficient allocation only when markets are operating in a perfectly competitive environment. This implies that (a) price levels in both factor and product markets are determined by the forces of demand and supply, (b) firms move easily into and out of any sector with perfect factor mobility to ensure an optimal use of resources, (c) no configuration other than the price mechanism assumes the role of rationing resources, and (d) commodity prices reflect the opportunity cost of the factors employed in their production. Absent any one of the conditions characterizing perfect competition, the market fails to achieve efficiency.

Market Failure

One major source of market failure is imperfect information. Normally, relevant information is hard to obtain and sometimes does not exist; even if it does exist, individuals may be unaware of its availability. This poses a limitation for individual maximization behavior to the extent that information is not available for making rational decisions.

Imperfect competition and externalities are additional sources of market failure. Various barriers blocking entry to an industry may exist or may result from monopolistic practices. Such barriers constrain output levels, keep prices above their competitive levels, and thus lead to an inefficient allocation of resources. When externalities are present, the marginal cost excludes the costs imposed on third parties, or the market demand leaves out the social benefits. Either way, social marginal cost deviates from social marginal benefit, leading to a misallocation of resources.

Another source of market failure is the market's inability to allocate resources in the public sector. Because they serve both individual and collective needs, public goods require collective decision making for their provision. Unlike a private good, once a public good has been produced, it becomes available to everyone at a given quantity, whatever the price that individuals wish to pay. The link between willingness to pay and the benefits expected (an important feature upon which the concept of efficiency is based in the case of private goods) thus breaks down, raising the need for an alternative theoretical framework to examine the efficiency question in the public sector.

These real-world conditions distort the working of the price mechanism and cause the market to deviate from its ideal efficiency level. Because the main impact is on the price structure, all of these imperfections generate a divergence between observed prices and production costs in both factor and product markets, causing under- or overutilization of resources.

The extent of the deviation is minimal only when price distortions and their resource allocation implications are inconsequential. Normally, when this is the case, price and profits reflect the real scarcity values of society's resources and accurately direct their intra-industrial movements; therefore, corrective measures are not needed. However, when a market economy significantly departs from this ideal setting, government involvement becomes necessary. Besides its traditional function of public good provision, government forms public policies, particularly in those areas where the market fails to direct resources to their optimal uses.

SUMMARY

Pareto optimality is an economic efficiency criterion indicating a state of economic affairs in which no one can be made better off without simultaneously making one other person worse off. Describing the conditions that must be met to achieve Pareto optimality, this chapter showed that (a) for both production and exchange efficiency to be achieved, the rate at which two commodities are substituted in production must equal the rate at which they are exchanged in consumption; (b) in a two-good and two-individual world, there exist an infinite number of allocations satisfying Pareto efficiency; and (c) from all possible Pareto-optimal allocations, the socially most desirable allocation is at the point of tangency between the highest attainable social indifference curve and the grand utility frontier.

When operating in a perfectly competitive environment, markets attain Pareto optimality. Through the interaction of supply and demand, the market mechanism produces a set of prices that satisfies the efficiency conditions. However, markets fail to achieve efficiency when faced with the problems of imperfect information, monopoly, externalities, and public goods. The resulting price distortion in each case causes over- or underutilization of resources.

The next chapter reexamines the efficiency concept in relation to the public sector. It outlines the conditions that need to be satisfied to achieve optimality and shows the extent to which actual resource allocations may diverge from the ideal allocations in the public sector.

APPENDIX:
PRODUCTION AND EXCHANGE EFFICIENCY CONDITIONS

Pareto optimality requires three conditions: (a) production efficiency, which ensures the equality of the marginal rate of technical substitution between the two factors of production in all sectors; (b) exchange efficiency, which requires the marginal rate of substitution between two goods to be the same for all individuals; and (c) allocative efficiency, which requires the rate at which two goods are substituted in production to be equal to the rate at which they are exchanged in consumption.

Production Efficiency Condition

To envision production efficiency, consider a two-sector model consisting of two goods (X and Y); two factors, capital (K) and labor (L); and two production functions

$$X = f(K_X, L_X) \tag{2A.1}$$

$$Y = f(K_Y, L_Y). \tag{2A.2}$$

In this model, capital and labor can be employed in various proportions with output levels remaining unchanged in both sectors or rising in one sector at the expense of the other. As described by the isoquants in Figure 2A.1 (drawn for good X), the same amount of X can be produced by using various combinations of capital and labor. As the factor combination varies along the isoquant, the output level remains the same. For example, the labor/capital combinations at points h and i yield the same output X_1. Also, when capital is used more intensively in X, less of it becomes available for the production of Y, and the employment of more labor in Y leaves less labor for X. Thus,

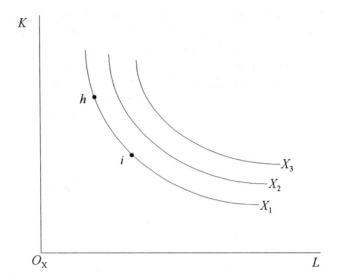

Figure 2A.1. Isoquants.

Note. The same amount of X can be produced by using various combinations of capital and labor. The factor combination varies along an individual isoquant, but the output remains the same. Points h and i represent the quantity of output X_1 at different proportions of labor and capital. X_2 represents a higher level of output than X_1, and X_3 is higher than both X_2 and X_1.

assuming that resources can flow freely between the two sectors, factor movement between X and Y could result in increased output in both sectors or in one sector without reducing output in the other.

If factor movements lead to a production stage where the output of X can be increased only by reducing the output of Y, then efficiency in production has been achieved. In technical terms, such a stage is reached when K and L are allocated between two goods X and Y such that

$$\text{MRTS}_{LK}^X = \text{MRTS}_{LK}^Y \qquad (2A.3)$$

or

$$(\text{MP}_L/\text{MP}_K)^X = (\text{MP}_L/\text{MP}_K)^Y. \qquad (2A.4)$$

MP_L and MP_K are the marginal products of L and K, respectively. MRTS_{LK} is the *marginal rate of technical substitution* of labor for capital, which is the

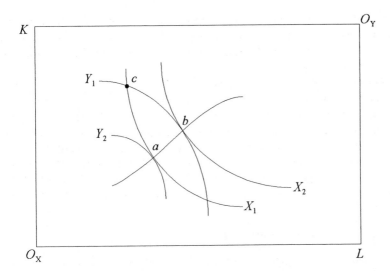

Figure 2A.2. The tangency between two sets of isoquants.

Note. At points a and b, further rearrangements of L and K result in an increase in the output of one at the expense of the other. Point c is inefficient because a movement to a will increase the output of Y while keeping the output of X unchanged; likewise, a movement to b will increase the output of X while keeping the output of Y unchanged.

amount of additional L required to compensate for a marginal decrease in K and still maintain the same level of output.

Production efficiency defined in these terms is described in Figure 2A.2 by an Edgeworth box diagram, where the horizontal and vertical axes represent the total quantities of labor and capital, respectively. The output X is measured from the origin of the bottom left corner, O_X, and the output Y is measured from the origin of the top right corner, O_Y. The initial allocation at point c represents the K/L employed in X and Y. A change in K/L from c to a raises the output of Y while keeping the output of X unchanged. Note that as we move from c to a, we remain on the same isoquant X_1 for X, but we move to a higher isoquant Y_2 for Y. Similarly, a change from c to b raises the output of X while keeping Y unchanged. Only at a and b, where the isoquants are tangent, do further rearrangements of L and K result in an increase in the output of one at the expense of the other. These are the points where the MRTS of L for K for both goods are equal.

The reallocation of factors of production and the resulting changes in the output of X and Y also can be described by the production possibilities curve PP introduced above in Figure 2.1. This curve is derived from the contract curve, which is the locus of all efficient points (the tangency points between the two sets of isoquant maps) at given quantities of K and L. It illustrates the maximum amount of X and Y that could be produced with a given resource base and technology.

Allocations represented by points below the frontier present an infinite number of possibilities available to raise total output without requiring additional resources. By reallocating resources from c to either a or b, output can be raised in one sector without reducing output in the other. A movement from a to b results in increased output of X and reduced output of Y.

Note that as factors are transferred from a to b, MRTS_{LK}^{X} and MRTS_{LK}^{Y} remain equal. Only the rate at which Y is converted into X, which is called the marginal rate of transformation of Y for X (MRT_{XY}), varies.

Exchange Efficiency Condition

The condition for exchange efficiency is illustrated by a two-sector model with two utility functions

$$U^{A} = U^{A}(X, Y) \qquad (2A.5)$$

$$U^{B} = U^{B}(X, Y) \qquad (2A.6)$$

The utility that A and B derive from alternative combinations of X and Y is represented by the indifference curves shown in Figure 2A.3. An indifference curve represents all possible combinations of X and Y among which the individual is indifferent. Every point along an indifference curve provides the same level of satisfaction, and each curve corresponds to a different level of satisfaction. For example, the combination of X and Y at point j provides the same utility as the combination at point k; but point m represents a higher level of utility than do j and k.

Note that with a move from j to k, utility remains the same, but the rate at which X and Y are substituted varies. The rate at which X is substituted for Y, which is called the marginal rate of substitution of X for Y (MRS_{XY}), varies as we move along the indifference curve.

To achieve exchange efficiency, the following condition must be met:

$$\text{MRS}_{XY}^{A} = \text{MRTS}_{XY}^{B}. \qquad (2A.7)$$

This equality represents the tangency between the two indifference curves depicted in Figure 2A.4. This time, the axes of the Edgeworth box shown in

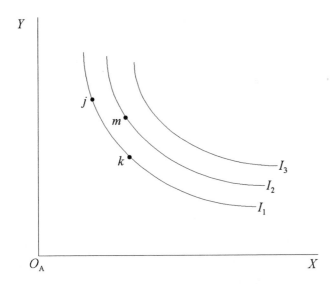

Figure 2A.3. Indifference curves.

Note. Each curve shows all combinations of X and Y that yield the same utility. Points j and k provide the same utility to the individual, but point m represents a higher level of utility than do j and k. With a movement from j to k, utility remains the same; however, the rate at which X and Y are substituted varies.

the figure represent outputs X and Y, with consumption levels of A and B measured from the origins O_A and O_B, respectively.

Both individuals gain from the reallocation of goods from an initial allocation point d to e or h. As a result of the reallocation from d to e, individual A remains on the same indifference curve, whereas individual B moves to a higher indifference curve (from B_1 to B_2). Similarly, a reallocation from d to h benefits A with no change in B's utility. At the tangency points, MU_X/MU_Y is equal for both individuals.

This situation and other combinations leading to the same equality are depicted in Figure 2A.4 by the contract curve. This curve is the locus of all possible combinations of X and Y that can be allocated between A and B at one particular output level. Each point on the contract curve satisfies the exchange efficiency condition, and any movement between two points results in redistribution, benefiting one individual at the expense of the other. Points below or above the contract curve, on the other hand, represent inefficiency because more can be gained from a given bundle of goods by moving toward the curve. Thus, all movements other than those toward the contract curve are inconsistent with Pareto optimality.

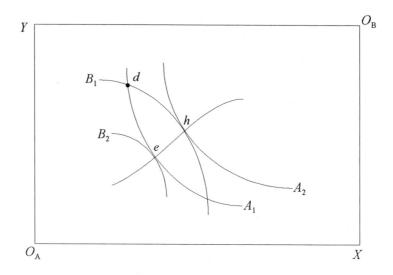

Figure 2A.4. The tangency between two sets of indifference curves.

Note. Individuals gain from a reallocation of goods from d to e or h. At the tangency points e and h, MU_X/MU_Y is equal for both individuals.

Allocative Efficiency Condition

The allocative efficiency condition is satisfied when the rate at which commodities are substituted in production equals the rate at which they are exchanged in consumption. To graphically trace the derivation of such allocations, (a) we begin with a production possibilities frontier that depicts all possible points of production efficiency (Figure 2.1); (b) we illustrate all possible points of exchange efficiency for a particular output combination by drawing a contract curve (Figure 2A.4); and (c) from an infinite number of contract curves, each corresponding to a different point on the production possibilities curve, we draw a grand utility frontier (Figure 2.2) depicting only those points that are efficient in both production and exchange.

NOTES

1. For references and further reading on Pareto optimality, see Bator (1957), Boadway and Wildasin (1984, chap. 2), and Ng (1979, chap. 2).

2. Alternative combinations yielding the same utility are described with an indifference curve. As discussed in the appendix to this chapter, an indifference curve represents all possible combinations of two commodities among which the individual is indifferent. For more on the indifference curve, also see the appendix to Chapter 5.

3. This situation and other combinations leading to the same equality can be shown by a contract curve, which illustrates all possible combinations of X and Y that can be allocated between A and B at one particular output level. Every point on the production curve coincides with a separate contract curve. See the appendix to this chapter.

4. Details of the derivation are provided in the appendix to this chapter. For a more comprehensive discussion, readers may also refer to Bator (1957) and Boadway and Wildasin (1984).

5. Note that when compensation is actually carried out, the project also satisfies the Pareto rule. In this case, both A and B are better off. For more on this, see Stokey and Zeckhauser (1978, 279-80). Also, for a detailed discussion of the differences between and policy relevance of Pareto and potential Pareto rules, see Griffin (1995).

6. This function, first used by Abram Bergson and alternatively referred to as the Bergson-Samuelson social welfare function, is widely used in economic analyses involving distributional issues. For details, see Tresch (1981, chap. 2).

DISCUSSION QUESTIONS

1. Describe the criteria by which economists judge the private market's performance in achieving optimality in resource allocation.

2. Use a production possibilities curve to describe all possible allocations that satisfy production efficiency. Will production efficiency alone be a sufficient condition for Pareto optimality? Explain.

3. Explain the differences between the production possibilities frontier and the grand utility frontier. Which of these frontiers is a depiction of the allocative efficiency condition?

4. What is the main difference between Pareto improvement and potential Pareto improvement? Which one of these efficiency interpretations is more relevant in real-world situations?

5. Pareto optimality is achieved when all three conditions for efficiency are satisfied. Does this mean that social welfare is also maximized? Explain.

6. Describe the circumstances under which a market economy can achieve a Pareto-optimum allocation. Could these circumstances also lead to a welfare maximum outcome?

3

Market Failure, Economic Efficiency, and Collective Decision Making

As explained in the preceding chapter, markets in the real world may fail to achieve economic efficiency for a number of reasons, including the market's inability to adequately provide for collective goods, the presence of externalities, and society's tendency toward imperfect competition. The source of inefficiency in each case is the deviation of the marginal social benefit from the marginal social cost of the output. For example, because of the free rider problem, the total amount that individuals are willing to pay for a public good may be too small to justify its provision. If the output is produced at a level that satisfies only the needs of those individuals who have revealed their willingness to pay for the good, then the marginal social benefit will deviate from the marginal cost of the good, leading to underutilization of resources. Similarly, when negative externalities are present, the marginal private cost excludes the costs imposed on nonconsenting third parties, or, as in the case of positive externalities, the marginal private benefit leaves out the external benefits. Marginal social cost in either case deviates from marginal social benefit, leading to over- or underproduction and thus misallocation of resources. A similar situation exists in the case of monopoly. At the profit-maximizing output level, market price exceeds marginal cost, and that results in a lower-than-competitive output level.

Price distortions caused by government's financing and spending decisions also result in misallocation of resources. Government's spending and taxation policies usually interfere with the workings of the price mechanism and change the nature of decision making in the private market. For example, the introduction of an energy tax as part of a deficit reduction package is likely to be distortionary because the tax will cause the benefit of using one additional BTU to exceed its marginal cost. Such deviation could change the composition of production and consumer spending in the energy sector and cause inefficiency in the economy because of resource reallocation based on distorted market dynamics. When viewed from this perspective, government policies are rarely neutral; taxation and spending measures distort price ratios and consequently cause individuals to alter their decision-making behavior.

Despite these distortionary effects, governments, as collective decision-making entities, work toward achieving social outcomes that are unattainable through market forces. Two primary goals of government are improving economic efficiency in resource allocation and achieving a welfare level based on society's distributional norms. In addition to its role of providing the necessary collective goods, government sets standards and regulations to promote economic efficiency and redistributes income to improve social welfare.[1]

This chapter focuses on three areas of government involvement in the private market: public goods, externalities, and imperfectly competitive market structures. For each of these areas, it examines the concept of economic efficiency and describes the circumstances under which efficiency is attained. The chapter also provides a brief discussion of some of the collective decision-making rules relevant to public expenditure analysis.

EFFICIENCY IN THE PRESENCE OF PUBLIC GOODS

Public goods have two fundamental characteristics: (a) They are nonrival in consumption, and (b) exclusion is either impossible or very costly. Consumption is *nonrival* when one individual's consumption does not prevent others from consuming the same commodity.

For example, a public radio program, once on the air, is available to every individual. One person's tuning in does not prevent others from listening to the same program. Similarly, public information provided by federal agencies on issues such as health, environment, and product safety regulations is available to all citizens; there will be no change in its availability as more individuals share such information. Once these goods have been produced, one more person's consumption raises total consumption benefits in a community, and, assuming that congestion costs are negligible, the cost of providing these goods to an additional individual is zero. Therefore, because the net social benefit from an additional individual's consumption is positive, excluding that individual from consumption of the public good will not be efficient.

Applying the *exclusion principle* to public goods is also technically infeasible. Because these goods are available to everyone in a community, excluding those individuals who are unwilling to pay for them would be impractical and costly to monitor. For example, preventing access to an uncrowded public park would require construction of a gate, a fence to exclude the nonpayers, and a guard to screen visitors. As another example, denying police protection to individuals who are exempted from local taxes (or have chosen to avoid taxes) would be impractical because screening procedures to exclude the nonpayers would be too costly. Exclusion could be workable for some congestible public goods, such as crowded highways, bridges, public beaches, and so on. But in the case of pure public goods, exclusion is impractical and infeasible.

Efficiency Conditions for Pure Public Goods

To examine the efficiency conditions in the presence of a public good, consider the traditional demand and supply curves depicted in Figure 3.1. The supply curve S_Z indicates the marginal cost of producing additional quantities of a public good Z; the demand curve D_Z depicts the quantities of Z that a community is willing to have at alternative costs. Assuming it is a small community with three income groups (or three individuals, for simplicity), the demand schedules, d_A, d_B, and d_C represent individuals' willingness to pay for alternative quantities of the good. At equilibrium, the price of the

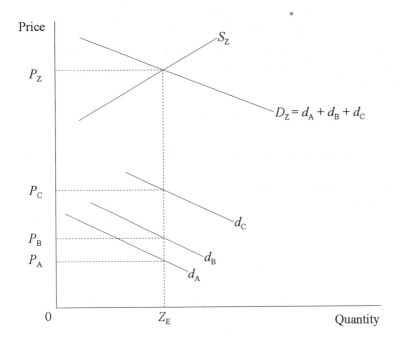

Figure 3.1. Demand and supply of public good Z.

Note. D_Z depicts the quantities of Z that a community is willing to have at alternative prices, whereas S_Z indicates the marginal cost of producing additional quantities of Z. Demand schedules d_A, d_B, and d_C represent the individuals' willingness to pay for the public good. At the equilibrium, P_Z is the total of P_A, P_B, and P_C, and it indicates the dollar amount that society is willing to pay collectively for Z_E.

good (P_Z) is the total of individual prices P_A, P_B, and P_C, and it indicates the dollar amount that society is willing to pay collectively for quantity Z_E. As illustrated in the figure, for the equilibrium quantity Z_E, individuals *A, B,* and *C* are willing to pay P_A, P_B, and P_C, respectively.

Note that for private goods, the market sets the price, and individuals decide how much to consume at that price, but in the case of public goods, the community decides how much to pay for a collectively determined quantity. In other words, the demand curve of a private good is derived by horizontally adding individual curves; but as shown in Figure 3.1, the demand curve of a public good is derived vertically, adding all three demands d_A, d_B, and d_C at each quantity.

Another distinction between private and public goods relates to the efficiency conditions. As shown in the previous chapter, the efficiency condition for private goods requires that each individual's marginal benefit equals the market price. In the case of three individuals, this is described as

$$MB_A = MB_B = MB_C = P_X , \qquad (3.1)$$

where MB is the marginal benefit and P_X is the price of the private good.

Efficiency in the presence of a public good, on the other hand, would require the fulfillment of both the aggregate efficiency condition and the marginal efficiency conditions. These are

$$\sum MB = MC = P_Z \qquad (3.2)$$

and

$$MB_A = P_A$$

$$MB_B = P_B \qquad (3.3)$$

$$MB_C = P_C.$$

According to the aggregate efficiency condition (3.2), the cost of producing Z_E must equal the sum of individual payments for the good, and that in turn must equal the sum of individual benefits. The marginal efficiency conditions (3.3) require each individual's evaluation of Z_E to equal the dollar amount that the individual is willing to pay.

Thus, considering both (3.2) and (3.3), Pareto efficiency in the public sector is theoretically possible. In addition to optimal provision of the good, which satisfies (3.2), the method of financing the good is also compatible with the free market solution, which is what is implied by (3.3). Under a voluntary financing scheme such as this, each individual is contributing according to his or her own marginal evaluation, and the payments received from all individuals combined total P_Z. This form of financing is known as the Lindahl tax share system, named after economist Erik Lindahl.

It should be noted, however, that in real-world situations, an efficient amount of a public good may not be produced because of inadequate preference revelation. There may be a tendency for individuals to become free riders by concealing their true preferences for the good and avoiding payments, especially when the good is provided through voluntary financing. When that is the case, the sum of revealed preferences may be too small to justify provision of the good. Sometimes, the public good may be produced but in insufficient amounts. The sum of private marginal benefits may be such that it can only justify an output level satisfying the demand of those who have revealed preferences. But because the marginal social benefit (including the benefits of nonpayers) will exceed the marginal cost of the good, not enough will be produced, and, therefore, such an allocation would lead to underutilization of resources in the public sector. This is when compulsory finance in public goods provision becomes an issue.

Compulsory Finance. According to the analysis above, projects designed to produce public goods pass the Pareto efficiency test only when the Lindahl tax share system is operative; that is, in addition to the aggregate efficiency condition, the individual payments for the good (the tax shares) must also be in line with voters' preferences. Alternatively, the tax shares can be determined at equal amounts for all voters, as is the case in most real-world situations. With this solution, each voter is charged the same amount toward the financing of the public good introduced at a quantity Z_E (Figure 3.2).

At Z_E, each voter contributes $\frac{1}{3}$ of the cost of the public good; at this tax price P_t, only B's marginal efficiency condition is satisfied. This is because Z_E corresponds to the point where B's marginal benefit from the public good equals P_t.

Individuals A and C also benefit from the project. These gains are shown in the graph by the vertical distance between P_t and A's and C's prospective demands as the quantity of the public good is first raised to Z_1 and then to Z_E. Note, however, that as the output is raised from Z_1 to Z_E, A is also incurring a loss: At Z_E, A's most preferred outcome would have been achieved at a lower tax share, but at price P_t, he is, in effect, incurring a loss amounting to area L. Also, C's most preferred outcome would have been attained at a tax share higher

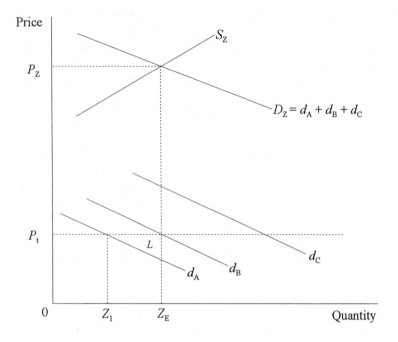

Figure 3.2. Equal tax share financing of a public good.

Note. At Z_E, each voter contributes one third of the cost of the public good, and at this tax price P_t, only B's marginal efficiency condition is satisfied. As output is raised from 0 to Z_1, all three individuals gain; from Z_1 to Z_E, B and C gain, whereas A incurs a loss shown by area L.

than P_t. Overall, however, the project is considered feasible: At Z_E, the aggregate efficiency condition is satisfied, and the net gain (the surplus gains of all three individuals minus A's losses) exceeds zero.[2]

Notice that the outcome in Figure 3.2 is not efficient in a strict Pareto optimality sense. As output is raised from Z_1 to the equilibrium welfare position Z_E, both B and C gain, whereas A incurs losses. Such an allocation is a potential Pareto improvement in the sense that implementation of the project could be made possible by having both C and B transfer a portion of their gains to A. Even if the transfer of gains does not take place, the project still meets the potential Pareto criterion as long as the resulting gains exceed the losses. The preceding analysis clearly shows that efficiency in the presence of public goods, in both the Pareto optimal and the potential Pareto sense, is possible.

Which of these two rules is more applicable to cost-benefit analysis (CBA)? When we consider that the fundamental principle of CBA is to select a project with the highest net return to society, both seem to be suitable as long as the net benefits are positive. The use of Pareto optimality is more limited, however, because the project will be acceptable only if it improves the well-being of at least one individual without making someone else worse off. As a decision rule this is very restrictive, and it will be applicable only if those who gain from the project do, in fact, compensate those who lose. In most situations, however, transfers of income intended to satisfy the strict Pareto rule may not be practical. Not only will it be difficult to devise a system of compensation because of the diffused nature of some welfare losses, but also there will be additional transaction costs that could outweigh the net project benefit. So, in real-world applications, the potential Pareto rule is more convenient to use because it will be sufficient to select a project on the basis of the highest net benefit rule without worrying about whether compensatory payments need to be made.

EFFICIENCY IN THE
PRESENCE OF EXTERNALITIES

Externalities are costs and benefits imposed on third parties. They are unintentional, and their effects are not conveyed through the price mechanism. Examples of external costs, also called *negative externalities,* include costs associated with a variety of industrial air pollutants produced as part of the production process. When such externalities exist, firms are not held accountable for the damage they cause, production costs exclude the costs associated with the pollutants, and individuals subject to the externality may not be compensated for the damage inflicted on them.

The source of the problem in this or any other negative externality case is a resource for which ownership rights are either unclear, nonexistent, or unenforceable. For example, consider a production function

$$Q = f(K,L,E) , \tag{3.4}$$

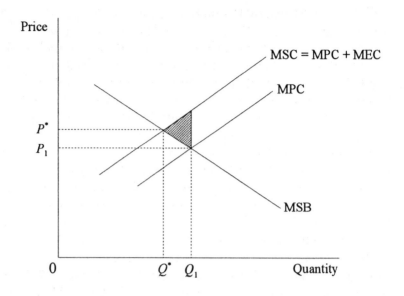

Figure 3.3. Overutilization of resources because of external costs.

Note. Marginal social cost (MSC), which include marginal private cost (MPC) and marginal external cost (MEC), exceeds marginal social benefit (MSB) at output level Q_1. The inefficiency created at this output level is shown by the shaded area. The optimal output from society's perspective is at Q^*.

where K is capital, L is labor, and E is a resource (such as air or a waterway) that is freely available to producers. Because E is free to producers (but not free from society's perspective), it is overutilized, and production is driven beyond its socially optimal level. As depicted in Figure 3.3, the marginal private cost (MPC) includes the cost of K and L and all other inputs for which producers make the required payments. The marginal external cost (MEC), which is the cost associated with the utilization of E, is not included in the MPC. Symbolizing the damage imposed on third parties that results from the utilization of E, MEC is included in the marginal social cost (MSC). As illustrated in the figure, MSC is equal to MPC plus MEC.

Note that the optimal output level from the firm's perspective is Q_1. This is the output level where MPC equals marginal social benefit (MSB), but it is also the output where MSC exceeds MSB, causing inefficiency in resource allocation. Ideally, the output should be at

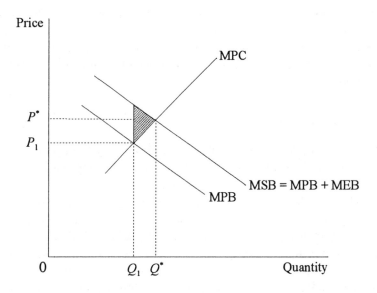

Figure 3.4. Underutilization of resources because of external benefits.

Note. Marginal social benefit (MSB), which includes marginal private benefit (MPB) and marginal external benefit (MEB), exceeds marginal private cost (MPC) at output level Q_1. The shaded area is the potential gain lost by not expanding output to the efficient level Q^*.

Q^*, where MSC intersects MSB, an equilibrium attained when producers are made liable for the damage caused.

In the case of external benefits, also called *positive externalities*, the source of inefficiency is underutilization of resources. As illustrated in Figure 3.4, social demand (MSB), incorporating both private demand (MPB) and the marginal external benefit (MEB), exceeds marginal private cost (MPC) at Q_1, causing an inefficient allocation of resources. The social loss in this case, which is associated with the output level produced to satisfy private demand, is the potential gain lost by not expanding the output to its socially desirable level. The magnitude of the potential gain, which is shown in Figure 3.4 by the shaded triangle, could be realized by expanding the output to the efficient output level Q^*.

Thus, for external costs as well as external benefits, the efficient output level Q^* is reached once the externality has been internalized.

In the case of external costs, this would mean that producers must either pay for the "free" resource or compensate for damages resulting from overutilization of the resource. In the case of external benefits, output is raised to its socially desirable level by using some form of subsidy or incentive plan.

Internalizing External Effects

Externalities can be internalized by mutual agreement among the parties involved or corrected through government intervention. Negotiation provides an efficient solution when the parties involved in an externality problem are few and negotiation costs are small. With this approach, individuals party to an externality problem reach a mutually agreeable outcome compatible with the free market solution.

Government intervention as an alternative becomes necessary only when negotiation fails to correct the problem. Through production standards, externalities are controlled by following certain procedures, such as installing emission control devices to reduce the likelihood of environmental damage; through corrective fees (known as Pigouvian adjustments) and marketable pollution permits, producers are also required or encouraged to move toward efficient output levels. Following is a discussion of each of these alternatives.

Internalization Through Negotiation. According to the Coase theorem, internalization of externalities can be achieved through private negotiation rather than government intervention.[3] As an example, consider a situation in which an industrial plant pollutes a nearby river.[4] In doing so, costs are imposed on a fisherman who uses the river. Assuming the plant owns the river, the fisherman will attempt to negotiate with the plant owner, hoping that the plant will agree not to overuse the river. Under the existing property rights, an optimal solution will be reached as follows: (a) negotiations will take place as long as the fisherman is willing to pay more than the plant's net gain from polluting the river, (b) the plant owner will be willing to reduce production as long as the compensation is greater than the net loss from doing so, and (c) the fisherman will be willing to pay as long as the compensation is less than the cost he incurs from polluted water. Through negotiations, a Pareto-optimal solution eventually will be reached.

It is important to note that for such negotiations to yield a feasible agreement, property rights do not have to be defined in favor of the plant. For example, the outcome will still be Pareto optimal if we now assume the fisherman has ownership rights to the river. Under this assumption, negotiations will take place as long as the plant owner is willing to pay more than the net gain to the fisherman if the river is used exclusively by the fisherman. The fisherman also will be willing not to fish as long as the compensation is greater than the net loss from not using the river. In either case, negotiations will produce an outcome that would be efficient in the Paretian sense.

In this and similar situations, it is clear that economic efficiency is likely to follow once the ownership rights to resources subject to externalities have been established. Individuals to whom these rights are assigned are expected to economize just as they would for all other private goods in their possession. Property rights may be assigned to specific groups or to society in general.[5] Either way, the outcome will be the same; individuals will allow their resources to be used as long as they receive adequate compensation. Resource ownership, private or collective, is therefore a prerequisite for efficient resource utilization.

In the preceding example, a private solution to the externality problem was feasible: Negotiating parties were few, and the transaction costs were assumed to be insignificant. However, as the number of nonconsenting third parties increases, transaction costs rise, and that, in turn, makes negotiations complicated and rather infeasible. For example, it will cost more time, effort, and money to reach a settlement between a steel company as the major source of air pollution in a large jurisdiction and the affected residents in that jurisdiction. In addition, the settlement between the affected parties will be complicated if the levels of exposure of both current and future generations to the contaminated environment vary significantly.

Even if the transaction costs are manageable or significantly low, there may still be a problem with preference revelation. For example, some affected individuals may choose not to participate in a legal action brought to ease the adversity of a contaminated environment, but they will still benefit from a judgment in their favor. This poses a free rider problem similar to that discussed in the case of public goods. When some individuals choose not to contribute to the cost of the suit, an insufficient amount of the good will be produced. In the case of air pollution, for example, this will mean less than the optimal level of pollution abatement.

Another problem with the private solution to the externality problem is distributional. As we stated above, the outcome of negotiation is always efficient regardless of how the property rights were initially assigned. What matters in negotiation, however, is who benefits from a private settlement and whether the settlement is in line with society's distributional norms. For these reasons and others, such as insufficient information about the level of exposure to the contaminated environment, disagreements concerning the severity of the problem, and ambiguities involved in the existing property rights legislation, internalization through government intervention becomes necessary.[6]

Internalization Through Government Intervention. Government can internalize external effects by setting production standards, imposing taxes and subsidies, or auctioning marketable pollution permits. As a procedure, setting production standards to reduce the likelihood of an externality problem is fairly straightforward. Certain standards are enforced by the government to restrict and monitor the level of pollution generated by producers. Alternatively, Pigouvian taxes and subsidies are assigned by government agencies to control external effects. Taxes are levied to minimize environmental damage in the case of air pollution, and subsidies are provided when output is below its socially desirable level, as in the case of making vaccines available to control communicable diseases.

To public economists, Pigouvian adjustments are more appealing than production standards because they are more in tune with free market solutions. In the case of negative externalities, where the source of the problem is the availability of an economic good at no cost to the user, the solution is to impose a fine or a tax that would require users to economize and treat the resource as a paid factor of production. In the case of positive externalities, benefits are generated for third parties, and to encourage optimal production of the good that generates the externality, a subsidy is provided as compensation.

With this approach, an optimal pollution abatement level can be achieved by either levying a Pigouvian tax or establishing pollution permits. The imposition of Pigouvian tax is shown in Figure 3.5. The

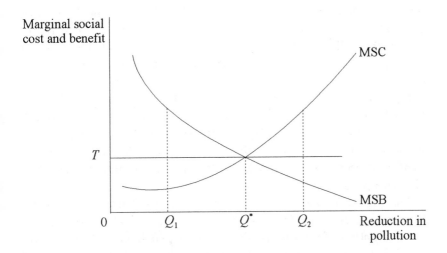

Figure 3.5. The optimal level of pollution abatement.

Note. Q^* represents the optimal level of pollution abatement where MSB intersects MSC. This level can be achieved by a corrective tax or a pollution permit. At Q_1, firms will be better off adopting a cleaner production process; at Q_2, they will be better off if they pay the tax or buy the permit.

downward sloping marginal social benefit (MSB) curve represents improved environmental quality. It is drawn on the assumption that recycling, disposing of, or cleaning up the first unit of pollution is socially more beneficial than doing so to the next unit. The marginal social cost (MSC) of additional reductions in pollution is depicted by an upward sloping curve. As the level of pollution abatement rises, foregone output, the loss of output that results from the use of environmentally sound production processes, rises as well.

The optimal level of pollution abatement for society is reached at Q^*, the point where MSB crosses MSC. This level is achieved by the corrective tax illustrated here by the horizontal line T. A tax imposed on the firm will be treated as the price of using the air to emit the waste and will force the firm to find the most efficient means of economizing on this paid resource. The firm will either pay the tax or search for efficient production alternatives to reduce the level of pollution. For example, at Q_1, firms will be better off if they use the production process to reduce the level of pollution, because at this level, the amount of the tax exceeds the value of foregone output because of the abatement policy. At Q_2, MSC exceeds the tax; therefore, firms will be better off if they pay the tax instead. The optimal level is achieved at Q^*, where the firms are indifferent between cleaning up and paying the tax.

Firms can also be driven toward Q^* by auctioning marketable pollution permits. With this market-based approach, firms bid for the right to pollute in amounts equal to the level set at Q^*. At the optimal price, which corresponds to the optimal pollution abatement level, firms have the choice of paying for the right to pollute or adopting a cleaner production process instead.[7]

The model displayed in Figure 3.5 forms the basis of most cost-benefit studies of environmental regulations. Typically, it is used for the evaluation of environmental programs, such as setting environmental standards, permits, and fines to achieve an efficient level of pollution abatement. Of particular importance is the benefit side of the model, for which various estimation techniques exist in the literature. As we discuss in Chapter 7, these include both direct and indirect methods for measuring the benefits of improved environmental quality.

One area of interest in cost-benefit studies has been in the area of environmental legislation. The Clean Water Act, for example, is one statute that recently has been capturing the attention of environmental economists. As the case study in Chapter 12 shows, benefits associated with water quality are quite diverse, including both use and nonuse benefits related to aquatic life, wildlife, and human health. These benefits are estimated and compared to the costs involved in complying with the water quality guidelines developed in accordance with the Clean Water Act.

EFFICIENCY IN THE
PRESENCE OF IMPERFECT COMPETITION

Before we discuss the efficiency conditions in the presence of imperfect competition, it is useful to review the price and output policy of a perfectly competitive market. As discussed in Chapter 2, output in perfect competition is determined where marginal cost

(MC) equals price. This is an output level where the resource value of an additional unit of output equals the market price, which reflects the consumer's evaluation of that additional unit of output. In the short run, average cost (AC), which is the total cost divided by the total output produced, may exceed or fall short of the market price, but in the long run, AC equals price. This means that although firms in a perfectly competitive environment may incur short-term economic profits (when price exceeds AC) or losses (when price is below AC), in the long run, they all approach output levels with zero economic profits. In this long-run setting, firms obtain a normal rate of return to all resources employed in production and remain in that setting until the rate of return begins to differ across industries.

Resources will move from one industry to another when profit levels begin to change because of price fluctuations. If a price increase in a particular industry results in relatively higher economic profits in that industry, it will lead to increased output and greater resource requirements. Consequently, both higher prices and higher profits attract the needed resources from other lower profit industries. Thus, whereas high profit industries begin to experience expansion, the lower productivity industries contract. This process of resource movement eventually leads to optimal resource allocation.

The price mechanism is rather limited in imperfectly competitive markets, where pricing and output policies are determined by one or a few firms. A distinguishing feature of imperfect competition is its pricing and output policy, which sets output at a level where market price exceeds MC. In contrast to perfect competition, where price equals marginal revenue (MR), in imperfect competition, price levels exceed their corresponding MR levels, and, therefore, at the equilibrium level of output, market price exceeds MC. This means that an imperfectly competitive firm—a monopolist, for example—sets its output at a level where market price, reflecting the consumer's evaluation of an additional unit of output produced, exceeds the resource value of that unit of output, thereby violating the allocative efficiency condition of Pareto optimality.

A monopolist will be able to maintain economic profits both in the short run and in the long run. Unlike perfect competition, profits will not approach their normal levels because of the existence of high barriers to entry. Because of these barriers, profit will remain in the

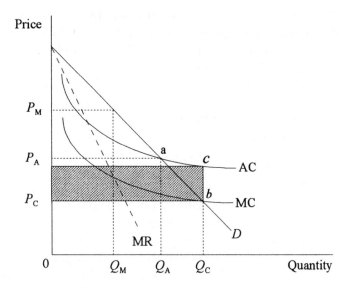

Figure 3.6. Output and pricing policies in natural monopoly.

Note. The profit maximization output for a natural monopoly corresponds to the point of inter-section between MC and MR. This output level is inefficient from society's perspective because at this output, consumers' evaluation of the good P_M exceeds the opportunity cost of producing the good MC. Efficiency can be attained at Q_C, but because of the losses shown by the shaded area, the monopolist will be reluctant to expand output to that level.

long run and thus will not play the role of coordinating the resource movement across industries as it does in perfect competition.

Natural Monopoly

Another problem relates to the size of the fixed costs. Firms, because of the nature of the industry, may require large fixed costs, as is the case in natural monopolies, such as highways, telephone companies, and public utilities. In these industries, the long-run average cost declines as output rises and exceeds MC at the point where MC crosses the demand curve. Also, the profit-maximizing output level corresponds to the point of intersection between MC and MR where price exceeds MC. As shown in Figure 3.6, the profit-maxi-mizing output for a natural monopoly is Q_M, and at this output level, the average profit is the difference between AC and the monopolist's price P_M.

Although Q_M is the most desirable output level from the monopolist's perspective, the resulting resource allocation is inefficient from society's perspective because at this output level, consumers' evaluation of the good exceeds the opportunity cost of producing the good ($P_M >$ MC). This, as described in Chapter 2, is a violation of the allocative efficiency condition.

Note that efficiency in the monopoly case could be attained only at production level Q_C, where MC intersects the demand curve. However, because of the losses shown by the shaded area, the monopolist will be reluctant to expand output to Q_C. This raises two options for the public policy maker: (a) force the monopolist to follow marginal cost pricing and compensate the monopolist for the resulting losses; or (b) regulate the monopolist through average cost pricing, which is commonly used in practice.

The first option is efficient in the potential Pareto sense because MC equals P_C, and the monopolist's loss may be transferred to the public sector through nondistortionary means. That is, government may choose to compensate the monopolist for its loss and do so by raising the required funds without creating inefficiencies elsewhere in society.[8] Alternatively, government could own the establishment and permit the management to follow MC pricing.

The second option, however, is not efficient in either the strict or the potential Pareto sense, but it is an improvement over monopolistic pricing. As shown in Figure 3.6, the price is set at P_A, where AC crosses the demand curve. At this price and corresponding output level Q_A, the efficiency loss is the distance between the demand curve and the MC curve over the relevant production range, and it is smaller than the efficiency loss under monopolistic pricing. A common practice in this approach is to also include in the AC a rate of return on the monopolist's investment, a rate regarded to be fair by regulatory agencies.

In concluding this section, it should be noted that determining the superiority of one option over the other would require a comparison of prospective benefits with transaction costs. Benefits would be efficiency improvements in resource allocation, and transaction costs would be the costs involved in developing and implementing various forms of regulatory procedures. These include AC and MC pricing as well as measures such as government taking over and managing natural monopolies.

Having analyzed the three primary market failures, described efficiency conditions in their presence, and reviewed their relevance to cost-benefit analysis, we now turn to the topic of collective decision making as the next step in the analysis of public sector expenditures. Topics that are essential to the analysis of public policy issues are briefly outlined to establish the theoretical basis for cost-benefit analysis in a collective decision-making environment.

COLLECTIVE DECISION-MAKING RULES

The public choice literature provides a variety of models to analyze the process of revealing collective preferences in democratic societies. These models can be classified into two broad categories of collective decision-making rules: (a) the absolute unanimity rule and (b) the simple majority rule.[9] Absolute unanimity is the direct application of the private market allocation system to the collective decision-making process; it requires 100 percent acceptance for a given measure to pass. Under the simple majority rule, on the other hand, a proposal only needs more than fifty percent of the votes to be approved.

Absolute Unanimity Rule

Individuals in a competitive market economy reveal resource allocation preferences through the price mechanism. They direct resources to specific uses by casting their "dollar votes" in the marketplace. This same procedure can be applied to the collective decision-making process, provided that individuals can reveal their true political inclinations in the same way they do for private goods. The absolute unanimity rule, which requires 100 percent acceptance for a given measure to pass, is analogous to the voluntary exchange solution of the market system.

To achieve overall efficiency in this context, both the aggregate and marginal efficiency conditions must be satisfied. As described in the preceding section, this means that

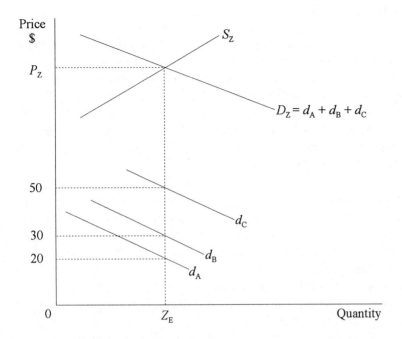

Figure 3.7. Aggregate and marginal efficiency conditions for political good Z.

Note. The aggregate efficiency condition is satisfied at output level Z_E. The marginal efficiency conditions are satisfied when individuals pay $20, $30, and $50, respectively.

$$\sum \text{MB}_i = \text{MC}, \qquad (3.5)$$

where MB_i is the marginal benefit to individual i from an additional quantity of a political good. In addition, the financing of the political good must be voluntary so that individuals voluntarily contribute an amount that maximizes their benefit from the political good. In a community of three individuals, A, B, and C, for example, every individual should pay Lindahl's tax price, which will satisfy the marginal efficiency condition. As depicted in Figure 3.7, the tax price will be different for each individual. In this example of a political good costing $100, the tax price is shown to be $20, $30, and $50 for individuals A, B, and C, respectively.

Simple Majority Rule

Although the simple majority rule is fairly straightforward, there are several issues that need to be clarified. These relate to (a) the question of political equilibrium and the percentage of votes that define a majority, (b) the relationship between individual political preferences and society's most preferred outcome, and (c) the problem of cycling, which may produce no decision under simple majority rule. Below, we briefly review some of the public choice models dealing with these issues.[10]

Optimal Voting Rule. This model is used to determine the voting rule that needs to be decided and written into the constitution in direct democracies.[11] It also provides a conceptual framework that may be used by decision makers to determine the optimal percentage of votes required to pass a proposal.

The optimal percentage that defines a simple majority is illustrated in Figure 3.8. The curve $C+D$ represents the cost of the decision-making rule, which consists of two cost functions: (a) the external cost function C and (b) the decision-making cost D. Externality costs, represented by the C curve, are those costs that are imposed on nonconsenting parties—individuals who do not favor a particular policy but are forced to participate in its financing. These costs will diminish as the percentage of individuals in a jurisdiction required for approval increases.

Decision-making costs, represented by the D curve, include transaction costs stemming from lobbying and negotiation activities for the purpose of raising the proportion of consenting votes. These costs will tend to increase as the percentage of votes required for approval increases, and they will reach their highest level when unanimity is a requirement.

As depicted in Figure 3.8, the $C+D$ curve is derived by summing these two curves. The minimum point on this curve corresponds to the optimal proportion of votes needed to pass a proposal.

Majority Voting Model. This model is used to examine society's most preferred political outcome. An individual's most preferred political outcome is attained at the point where the marginal benefit received from a given quantity of public good equals the individual's tax share.

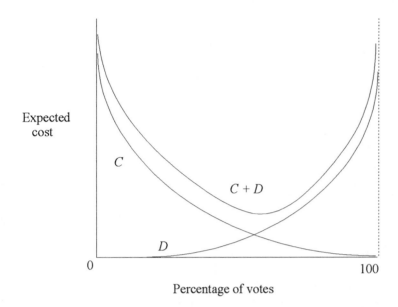

Figure 3.8. Optimal percentage of simple majority.

Note. Curve *C* represents costs on individuals who do not favor a policy but are forced to participate in its financing. *D* represents transaction costs related to lobbying and negotiation activities for the purpose of raising the proportion of consenting votes. The minimum point on the *C + D* curve corresponds to the optimal percentage that defines a simple majority.

Assuming that individuals decide in this manner, the votes that they cast for a proposal are likely to represent their most preferred outcomes, from which society's most preferred outcome is derived.

As an example of the majority voting model, consider a situation where three individuals are each asked to vote for one of three possible size capacities for a theme park. Suppose that the park can be built to accommodate 100, 200, or 300 visitors daily at a total cost of $150, $300, or $450, respectively. With each proposal supported by one of the three decision makers, the outcome according to the majority voting model is likely to be the decision corresponding to the median voter. As depicted in Figure 3.9, option *Y* (200 visitors), the median outcome, is the winner. In pairwise elections, *Y* will be the preferred size in two out of three situations, whereas *X* will be preferred in the third.

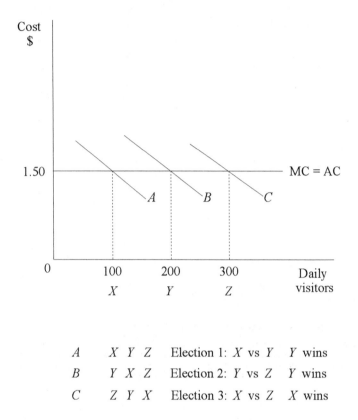

A	X Y Z	Election 1: X vs Y Y wins
B	Y X Z	Election 2: Y vs Z Y wins
C	Z Y X	Election 3: X vs Z X wins

Figure 3.9. Society's most preferred political outcome.

Note. With three decision makers, A, B, and C, supporting three proposals, X, Y, and Z, the outcome according to the majority voting model is likely to be what corresponds to the median voter. In pairwise elections, Y will be the preferred outcome.

The Problem of Cycling. The simple majority voting system may provide no winner in certain circumstances. This is the case when collective decisions made under simple majority rule become inconsistent or intransitive. This problem results from cycling, a situation of multipeaked preferences where pairwise elections produce no winner.

As an example of the cycling problem, assume each individual (A, B, and C) in the theme park example has a preference scale for each park size (100, 200, and 300). These preferences are tabulated next along with the results of pairwise voting. Because no single winner emerges from the elections, it is impossible to choose among the three alternative policies.

Voter	1st	Project Preferences 2nd	3rd
A	X	Z	Y
B	Y	X	Z
C	Z	Y	X
Election 1:	X versus Y	Y wins	
Election 2:	Y versus Z	Z wins	
Election 3:	X versus Z	X wins	

In this example, *B* and *C* have single-peaked preferences, whereas *A*'s preferences are multipeaked; unlike *B* and *C*, *A* moves from one extreme to the other. The solution to the cycling problem, therefore, is when all individuals' preferences are single peaked.[12]

From the preceding analysis it is clear that the simple majority rule would lead to society's most preferred outcome in any election as long as preferences are not multipeaked. It should also be noted that under the simple majority rule, society's most preferred political outcome is a potential Pareto optimum because the optimal proportion of votes needed to pass a proposal will include voters with potential gains and losses. The parallel solution in public finance is equal tax share financing, which was also shown to be a potential Pareto optimum. On the other hand, under the absolute unanimity rule, the outcome is optimum in a strict Paretian sense because the rule is a direct application of private market allocation and Lindahl's voluntary financing system.

SUMMARY

Government intervenes in the private economy whenever markets fail to achieve optimal use of resources because of the problems of imperfect competition, public goods, and externalities. In all of these cases, efficiency can be achieved if government intervenes in accordance with the free market solutions. In the case of monopoly, efficiency is attained when MC equals *P* and the resulting losses of the monopolist are compensated. In the public goods case, Pareto optimality is achieved when both aggregate and marginal efficiency conditions are satisfied. But when the financing scheme does not satisfy the marginal efficiency conditions, public good production still can be efficient in the potential Pareto sense as long as the aggregate efficiency conditions are satisfied. Finally, efficiency is also attained when Pigouvian taxes and subsidies are used to internalize externalities. Redefinition of property rights and negotiation in a small number and low transaction cost case are potential Pareto-efficient public policy remedies to control the externalities.

Government intervention in each case will produce potential gains and losses. Therefore, alternative forms of government regulations in the case of monopoly, different sizes of public goods provision in the case of public goods, and programs and various standards of pollution abatement all can be subjected to cost-benefit analysis. As also noted, cost-benefit techniques can be used in the legal system. However, for situations where property rights legislation involves society at large, public choice configurations probably would be more appropriate decision-making tools.

It should also be stressed that the decision rules in the public choice literature lay the theoretical foundation for public project analysis in a collective decision-making environment. As the rules and fundamentals of cost-benefit analysis are developed in subsequent chapters, it will be apparent that the public policy environment and the principles of public finance, as well as the public choice configuration, will have an important impact on the outcome of public expenditure analyses.

NOTES

1. As noted in Chapter 1, n. 4, government also performs a stabilization function, which is beyond the scope of this book.

2. For a thorough discussion of the gains and losses, see Gramlich (1990, 33-5).

3. In a seminal article, Ronald Coase (1960) argued that externalities can be internalized by establishing property rights to resources subject to externalities. In a small-number and no-transaction-costs case, efficiency is attained as long as one of the parties is granted the property rights.

4. For a detailed discussion of this classic example, see Rosen (1995, chap. 6).

5. In public project analysis, the existing set of property rights law is assumed to be given. But whenever changes in the existing law are considered, CBA can be employed to compare the benefits and costs of proposed changes. Benefits will be expected improvements in resource allocation measured in terms of additional welfare gains. Costs will include time and money costs involved in preparing, campaigning, and legislating such measures, plus litigation costs once such changes become part of the judicial process.

6. For more on the failures of private solutions to the problem of externality, see Stiglitz (1988, chap. 8).

7. The market permit approach is as efficient as Pigouvian adjustments. For more on both approaches, see Nelson (1987) and Johansson (1993, chap. 11).

8. However, this is unlikely because all forms of taxation in reality are distortionary; that is, they generate deadweight losses elsewhere in the economy. For more on this and the evaluation of other options to regulate the natural monopolist, see Rosen (1995, 335-9), Stiglitz (1988, chap. 7), and Boadway and Wildasin (1984, 171-6).

9. There is also the plurality rule, under which a candidate with the most votes wins. For example, in an election with more than two candidates, a candidate may be elected with less than fifty percent of the votes. For more on the plurality rule and its extensions and other alternative voting rules, see Levin and Nalebuff (1995).

10. For a detailed discussion of voting models, see Boadway and Wildasin (1984, chap. 6), and for a review of the literature, also see Mueller (1976).

11. See Buchanan and Tullock (1965, chap. 6) for details.

12. Kenneth Arrow was the first to establish that single-peaked preferences lead to consistent simple majority ranking. Recognizing that a similar conclusion was reached by Duncan Black (1948), Arrow gave the credit to Black for this very important solution to the voting paradox. For more on this, see Sen (1985, 1764-76).

DISCUSSION QUESTIONS

1. Is economic efficiency possible in the presence of market failures? Explain.

2. In which specific areas does government intervene in the private economy? What is the economic rationale underlying its involvement? Does government intervention introduce additional distortions to those already existing in the private market?

3. Describe the source of inefficiency in the case of natural monopoly. Can this problem be corrected? Under what circumstances can economic efficiency be achieved?

4. What are the main characteristics of a public good? How does a public good differ from a private good?

5. Briefly describe the efficiency conditions in the case of public goods, and show how a voluntary financing scheme differs from equal tax share financing. Which one of these financing schemes is more in line with a free market solution? Explain why.

6. What is the source of inefficiency in the case of negative externalities? Is efficiency possible in their presence?

7. Outline the three procedures suggested in the text to internalize external effects. Which of these procedures would lead to a free market solution?

8. Internalizing through negotiation is more appealing to economists than internalizing through intervention. Is this statement true or false? Explain why.

9. Could internalization through intervention produce a Pareto-optimal outcome?

10. Briefly describe the alternative collective decision-making rules, and, for each rule, show if economic efficiency could be achieved.

4

Principles of Cost-Benefit Analysis

Viewing resource allocation issues in the context of welfare economics, the preceding two chapters described both the Pareto and the potential Pareto criteria in detail. It was shown that Pareto efficiency applies to reallocation decisions that improve social welfare if at least one individual is made better off and no one is made worse off. The potential Pareto condition, referred to as the Kaldor-Hicks rule, was shown to be a more practical standard because it justifies any reallocation as long as it raises net social benefits. A reallocation that improves social welfare could be at the expense of someone becoming worse off, but under the Kaldor-Hicks rule, as long as those who benefit could compensate those who lose, the reallocation decision is accepted as an improvement.

Both chapters also cited the presence of market failure as the main reason for government intervention in the private market. Any departure from the ideal decision-making environment justifies government intervention aimed at improving social welfare through the introduction of public programs. Possible scenarios were discussed to show how collective decisions could direct resources to their optimal use. An important conclusion of this discussion is that, in theory, every policy intervention aims at maximizing social welfare, thereby attaining equilibrium solutions similar to those reached in compliance with the Kaldor-Hicks rule.[1]

We now turn to the specific issue of project evaluation. A public project will likely affect the welfare of three groups: those individuals who will be the beneficiaries of the project, taxpayers who will be providing the funds for the project, and those individuals who will be incurring losses once the project has been implemented. The analyst's main job is to identify these affected parties, calculate their losses and gains, and determine if the project is viable from society's perspective.

This chapter provides an overview of the CBA methodology. It begins with an example of a real-world application, followed by an outline of the main steps involved in a typical evaluation. The chapter also highlights the essential features of cost-effectiveness analysis—a methodology particularly useful when project benefits cannot be measured in dollar terms.

A TYPICAL COST-BENEFIT DESIGN

Implementing a new public project requires inputs that are either newly produced or drawn from other sectors of the economy. In a typical cost-benefit analysis, the social values of these inputs are assessed and compared to the dollar estimates of the total benefits that the project is expected to provide. The evaluation process consists of several stages, each paying attention to such details as totaling the benefits and costs accruing to different groups in different time periods, determining if the project will yield by-products that could generate additional losses and gains, weighing the gains and losses of different income groups, and considering many other factors that may have an impact on the decision of whether to implement a project. To keep matters simple, at this point, the focus is only on the main issue of determining the gains and losses to concerned parties in a given year.[2]

For illustration, consider a public project to improve the uncrowded shore of a small community by converting it into a public beach. The estimated cost of developing the beach is $150,000, and the future maintenance and operating costs are expected to be $15,000 annually. When completed, the beach will be provided free of charge to an estimated 15,000 individuals per year. Currently, 6000 individuals each year enjoy the existing facilities that are available for a variety of recreational activities, such as swimming, camping, and sailing at several locations along the shore. These facilities are serviced by the nearby private businesses, who charge a fee of $3 per visitor; the average cost is $2.50, and the average profit made by these businesses is $.50 per person.

To determine the feasibility of this project, the first step is to identify and calculate the net expected annual gains from its implementation. The annual benefits include two figures: (a) a gain of $18,000 ($3 × 6000) to the existing users, who will be able to use the parking facilities and services free of charge; and (b) a gain of $13,500 [½($3 × 9000)] to the new users, roughly estimated by the projected number of new visitors multiplied by the fee that they would have paid had there been a charge. The annual costs will also include two items: (a) a loss of $3000 [($3 − $2.50) × 6000] to the existing businesses because of the foregone profit of $0.50 per visitor, and (b) a loss of $15,000 to the taxpayers since tax money will be used for maintenance and operations.

Next, the yearly net benefits of $13,500 are calculated by subtracting the total annual losses of $18,000 ($3,000 + $15,000) from the total annual gains of $31,500 ($18,000 + $13,500). The present value of net benefits is then calculated and compared to the investment cost of $150,000. Leaving the details of the actual calculation to Chapter 8, the focus now is on the important issue of how to estimate the gains and losses associated with a project.

If the beach development had been a private project, the evaluation would have been rather straightforward. The analyst would have simply compared the cost of inputs, calculated by multiplying the quantity of resources used in developing the beach by their respective prices, to the revenue generated, which would be the projected number of visitors multiplied by the fee they would pay.

In the case of a public project, the analysis is more complicated for several reasons. For the most part, private projects are financed through individual payments for the product. A public good, on the other hand, requires public funds—revenues collected through taxes or other collective means—that are used to purchase the resources that need to be employed in the public project. Another important difference between public and private goods is that consumption of a public good is collective; that is, it is nonrival within a relevant output range, and the good in most situations may not carry a price tag. When that is the case, the analyst cannot use market data directly to determine the value that will be generated by the public good. For a product that is freely available to the community, there is no price and therefore no information on the public's evaluation of the good.

Note that in estimating the net benefits in this example, we calculated the benefits roughly by relying on a demand curve for the public good. In the case of a purely private good, this curve can be estimated from market data. For public goods, however, there is no fee charged for the service, and the good is funded collectively, so there is no reliable market data to estimate the curve. Therefore, a challenging task for the analyst is to determine individuals' preferences for this service within a wide range of beachgoers and, more important, to place a dollar value on these preferences. Before providing the details of some of the methods available for this purpose, we begin with an overview of the main steps involved in a typical cost-benefit analysis.

STAGES OF COST-BENEFIT ANALYSIS

Cost-benefit analysis proceeds in four essential steps: (a) identification of relevant costs and benefits, (b) measurement of costs and benefits, (c) comparison of cost and benefit streams accruing during the lifetime of a project, and (d) project selection.

Identification of Costs and Benefits

In the first phase of project analysis, all related costs and benefits are identified, and their relevance to a project is justified. A new project draws factors of production from other areas of employment. The transfer of these factors to the new project will generate new output and, at the same time, will result in output losses elsewhere in the economy. The task at this stage of the analysis is to identify these losses (costs) and estimate the value of the output (benefits) to be produced by the project.

The main reference in identifying costs and benefits is the Kaldor-Hicks efficiency standard. As discussed in Chapter 2, this standard is satisfied as long as a policy change maximizes net social benefits. According to this rule, those who benefit from an increase in output could compensate those who suffer from output losses and still remain better off.

To determine the net benefit of a policy change in this context, the gains and losses of all concerned parties need to be calculated, and for that, several conceptual distinctions must be recognized throughout the analysis. First, the analyst must distinguish costs and benefits that are *historical* from those that are *economic*. The former is a cost concept that has no relevance to resource allocation decisions involving the present or the future. For example, the cost incurred in building a recreation center is historical and thus should not enter into such decisions as whether to expand or demolish the center. Similarly, the cost of labor to a proposed project is not what the worker earned in the previous job. Rather, it is the output lost elsewhere in the economy as a result of the worker having relocated. The economic cost in either example is the value that the resource could generate in its next best use.

A related distinction is that between before-after and with-without approaches to net benefit assessment. The *before-after* approach is based on historical records of what costs and benefits were before the project and what they will be after the project. For example, a decline in the number of cancer cases would be inappropriately considered a benefit if the regulation to reduce exposure to asbestos is evaluated in the context of the before-after approach. An appropriate practice is to take the difference between the number of cases avoided because of the regulation and the number of cases that would have been observed without the regulation. This is the *with-without* approach commonly used in cost-benefit studies. Unlike the before-after approach, it compares the costs and benefits of a project in terms of the net marginal social utility that would have been gained with and without the project.

Another important distinction to be made is the difference between the real output effects and the pecuniary effects of a project. *Real output effects* are changes in total physical production possibilities with an ensuing change in society's welfare. *Pecuniary effects,* on the other hand, are distributional and create no real welfare gains to society. What might appear to be a real gain may, in fact, be pecuniary when there is a corresponding welfare loss elsewhere because of a project or a policy change. For example, the increase in property values following the relocation of a regional medical center to a small town is pecuniary and should not be counted as part of the real benefits of building the center. Such valuations may have been included already as part of the willingness to pay for the center in the new location, so the benefit generated is simply transferred to the homeowners. Therefore, adding the increased property values to the total benefits of the project will be double counting and should be avoided.

There are also issues with regard to drawing the jurisdictional boundaries of the analysis and distinguishing between tangible and intangible project outcomes. We return to a detailed discussion of these and other allocational issues in Chapters 5 through 7.

Valuing Costs and Benefits

Valuing costs and benefits is a demanding task that requires extreme care and creativity. Tangible elements of a project, such as capital equipment, labor, land, and so on must be priced, and values must be generated for intangibles and other categories of costs and benefits for which no price information exists.

Price information for tangible elements can be obtained easily from competitive markets. Normally, market prices represent economic values, but sometimes they need to be used with caution. In the absence of competitive market conditions, market prices are likely to misrepresent true scarcity values. For example, the market price of a project input may differ from its production cost, in part because of a distortionary tax. Because the difference between the market price and the production cost is considered a type of transfer payment, using the market price for a newly produced input is likely to overestimate the costs of the project. To avoid this problem, an adjusted price, called the *shadow price,* may be derived and, as will be shown in Chapter 6, used in measuring the costs and benefits of a project.

Another difficult problem is determining how to evaluate intangibles such as human life, time, morality, and environmental factors. For example, a project to expand a two-lane highway into four lanes may make a difference in terms of either loss of life resulting from increased traffic or time savings because of increased transportation efficiency. To determine the superiority of a four-lane highway over a two-lane highway, or to compare the transportation efficiency of both alternatives, it may be necessary to put a value on the number of lives that may be lost, as well as on time saved. This is not an easy task, and, as will be shown in Chapter 7, there are different views about how to deal with this problem.

Comparing Costs and Benefits

In the third phase of project analysis, the present value of future benefits and costs of a project must be calculated and compared to the present value of investment costs. To accomplish this, future net benefits are discounted by a factor. The critical issue at this stage is the choice of a discount rate. Normally, the rate used in cost-benefit analysis is different from that used in financial analysis. The latter is known as the market rate of interest, which is determined in the financial markets. This rate differs from the private rate of time preference when, for example, the loanable-funds market is distorted by government taxes. It also deviates from the social rate of time preference when society and the private market weigh investment differently.

Such variety of discount rates makes no difference in financial analysis. The purpose of any private project is to maximize private returns, and for that, the market rate of interest seems adequate. In public project analysis, however, the choice of a discount rate makes a difference because a public project is likely to show different benefit-cost ratios depending on the discount rate used. Because the implementation of a public project transforms present consumption into future consumption, it is important that such a transformation is done at a rate that is most desirable to society. Therefore, as will be described in Chapter 9, the market rate of interest may have to be adjusted to reflect society's preferences.

Project Selection

In the final stage of project analysis, projects are ranked in terms of at least one of the three project selection criteria. These include benefit-cost ratios, the net present value, and the internal rate of return. According to these criteria, a project is accepted when its benefit-cost ratio exceeds one, its net present value exceeds zero, and/or its internal rate of return is higher than the market rate or any other socially acceptable rate of return. Each of these criteria can be used to rank projects; but as will be shown in Chapter 8, projects may be ranked differently under different criteria and produce incompatible results.

COST-EFFECTIVENESS ANALYSIS

The preceding overview assumed that most of the information needed to conduct a reasonably complete cost-benefit analysis is available. The relevant costs and benefits in particular were assumed to be capable of being measured and compared in dollar terms. However, when the output of a project is undefined or cannot be measured in monetary units, cost-benefit analysis is of limited use. This is when analysts consider an alternative procedure known as cost-effectiveness analysis (CEA).

As an evaluation technique, CEA commonly is used either to select a project that would yield the least cost production of a given output or to choose a project that would yield the maximum output at a given cost. In the former case, the analyst ranks projects that are designed for the same outcome in terms of their costs. In the latter case, projects are ranked in terms of the quantities of output that they would yield given a fixed budget.[3]

The focus of CEA in either case is technological efficiency, and that is what makes CEA different from CBA.[4] In CBA, because benefits are assigned a monetary value, the main concern is economic efficiency. Other than this important distinction, the method of analysis used in CEA is essentially the same as that used in CBA.[5]

SUMMARY

This chapter provided an overview of the general methodology used in CBA and the main steps involved in the evaluation of a project. Costs and benefits are identified in reference to potential Pareto optimality and evaluated within the broader context of a policy and economic environment. An input of a project is defined as a cost if its employment in a project causes a loss of output elsewhere in the economy. An output is a benefit if it results in real welfare gains to society. To determine the real scarcity values for both inputs and outputs, cost-benefit measures are derived to correct for price distortions. Distortions result from possible market imperfections, such as externalities, distortionary taxes, and unemployment.

Costs and benefits that are difficult to quantify are also included in cost-benefit analysis. A significant portion of a project may consist of unquantifiable benefits and costs. These may include such intangibles as improved water and air quality, beautification of an environment, and improved quality of life. Although it is possible to measure intangibles in simple ratios or index numbers, as is the case in cost-effectiveness analysis, sometimes approximate dollar measures better serve the need to derive aggregate outcome measures. This latter type of quantification minimizes the complications that may result from using qualitative measures in producing a decision. Cost-benefit analysis allows for the derivation of quantitative measures to account for intangibles. Even if such measures are difficult or impossible to obtain, CBA still accounts for intangibles and includes them among other considerations that may affect the project's outcome.

The last stage of project evaluation involves discounting and project selection. An appropriate discount rate is selected and used to derive the net present value of the project.

NOTES

1. See Chapter 3 in Gramlich (1990) for more on the rationale of CBA and how it relates to welfare economics, microeconomics, and public choice.

2. An overview of CBA and a further discussion of issues involved at each stage of project evaluation can be found in Layard and Glaister (1994, 1-56).

3. Because output effects cannot be measured in monetary units, it is difficult to derive an appropriate benefit measure. Therefore, in CEA, various elements that enter an outcome measure of a project are defined and aggregated to form an overall effectiveness index. Note that the absence of a common denominator among these elements usually raises the need for weights in aggregating the output values. For more on this, see Tuckman and Nas (1980).

4. For a comparison of CEA and CBA, see McKenna (1980, chap. 7).

5. For more on CEA, see Guess and Farnham (1989, chap. 5), Warner and Luce (1982), and Mishan (1988, chap. 16).

DISCUSSION QUESTIONS

1. What are the primary criteria used in assessing the economic and social outcomes of government activities? Could such criteria be operational? How do we apply these criteria to specific government activities in cost-benefit analysis?

2. Think of an example of an imaginary public project and identify the parties who may gain or lose from the project if it is implemented. Would there have been a difference in your analysis if the project had been private?

3. Outline, and with one or two statements describe, each stage of cost-benefit analysis. Discuss some of the major issues that are raised at each stage of the analysis.

4. Can cost-benefit analysis be used in evaluating nominally unquantifiable output effects?

5. Explain how cost-effectiveness analysis differs from cost-benefit analysis.

6. Suppose you have a variable budget and a project with undefined or given benefits. What methodology would you suggest for evaluating the feasibility of the project? Can cost-benefit analysis be used? Explain.

5

Allocational Effects of Public Projects

This chapter discusses alternative measures of welfare change and explains how they are used to identify the net benefits of public projects. It begins with a brief description of the concept of consumer surplus, followed by a detailed discussion of compensating and equivalent variation measures of a welfare change. Using partial equilibrium analysis, the chapter also looks at the real output effects and the external effects of a project.[1] It stresses the point that these effects not only need to be properly identified and accounted for, but also must be distinguished from redistributive outcomes to avoid over- or understatement of costs and benefits.

CONSUMER SURPLUS

Consumer surplus is a monetary measure of the maximum gain that an individual can obtain from a product at a given market price. First introduced by Jules Dupuit in 1844 and later used by Alfred Marshall in 1920, the concept is defined as the difference between the maximum amount that an individual would be willing to pay for a good and the actual amount paid.[2]

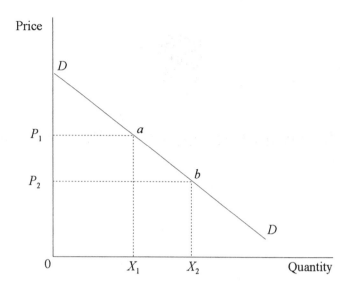

Figure 5.1. Measure of consumer surplus.

Note. $ODaX_1$ measures the maximum amount that the individual is willing to pay for X_1 units, and OP_1aX_1 is the amount that the individual actually pays at the market price P_1. The difference, P_1Da, is the consumer surplus. With a price decrease to P_2, the additional surplus gain is P_1abP_2.

As illustrated by the ordinary (Marshallian) demand curve DD in Figure 5.1, $ODaX_1$ indicates the maximum amount that the individual is willing to pay for X_1 units, and OP_1aX_1 is the amount that she actually pays at the market price P_1. The difference is the area P_1Da, representing the total value of the consumer surplus gained at X_1.

At a lower price, P_2, the consumer surplus corresponds to the area within triangle P_2Db, which is larger than triangle P_1Da. The difference between the two triangles, P_1abP_2, is the additional consumer surplus that results from the price decrease. As illustrated in Figure 5.2, the consumer surplus would be $2 when the individual acquires two units of a good at $6 each, assuming he or she would be willing to pay $8 for the first unit and $6 for the second. At a lower price, say $4, the individual will buy three units and the consumer surplus will rise to $6. The change in the consumer surplus in this example is $4.

Note that consumer surplus derived from an ordinary demand curve is not an exact measure of the welfare effect of a price change.

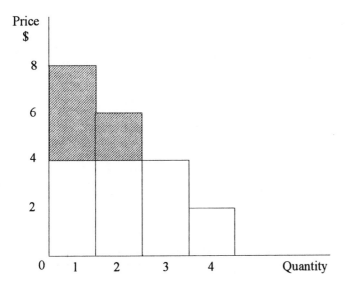

Figure 5.2. Consumer surplus.

Note. Consumer surplus would be $2 when the individual acquires two units of a good at $6 each. At $4, the individual will buy three units, and the consumer surplus will rise to $6. The change in consumer surplus is $4.

An ordinary demand curve assumes money income constant, and, consequently, its usefulness in CBA is questionable. By definition, a movement along the curve involves both substitution and real income effects, and when price decreases, both effects allow the individual to move to a higher indifference curve. Therefore, to obtain an exact measure of the welfare effect of a price change, we need to eliminate the real income effect and measure only the pure substitution effect of the price change.

To remove the income effect, we draw compensated demand curves, *HH* and *H'H'*, by allowing the individual to remain at the pre- and postprice change utility (real income) level (Figure 5.3). These curves (also called Hicksian demand curves) assume real income constant and account for the substitution effect of a price change alone. For normal goods, they have higher slopes than the ordinary demand curve, *DD*. The area under *DD*, P_1abP_2, represents the individual's evaluation of a price change as well as the change in the individual's

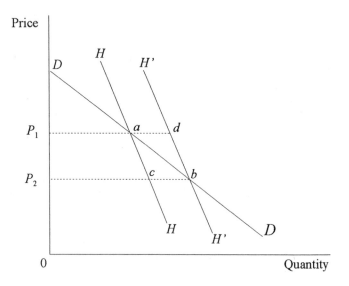

Figure 5.3. Measures of welfare change with Marshallian and compensated demand curves.

Note. The Marshallian curve is represented by DD and compensated curves by HH and $H'H'$. The area under DD, P_1abP_2, represents the individual's evaluation of a price change as well as the change in the individual's real income. The areas below the compensated curves account for the substitution effect only, and they are the precise measures of the variation in consumer welfare caused by a price change. When P_1 decreases to P_2, P_1acP_2 represents CV and P_1dbP_2 represents EV. When the price increases, CV and EV become P_1dbP_2 and P_1acP_2, respectively.

real income. The area below HH, P_1acP_2, and the area below $H'H'$, P_1dbP_2, account for the substitution effect only, and they are the precise measures of the variation in consumer welfare caused by a price change.

COMPENSATING AND EQUIVALENT VARIATION

The compensated demand curves shown in Figure 5.3 correspond to both compensating variation and equivalent variation measures. *Compensating variation* (CV) indicates the amount that an individual would be willing to pay (accept) for a price reduction (increase) while maintaining the preprice change total utility level. In the case of a price decrease from P_1 to P_2, it is shown as the area P_1acP_2 below HH in Figure 5.3. For a price increase from P_2 to P_1, it is shown in the same figure as the area P_1dbP_2 below $H'H'$.

Equivalent variation (EV), on the other hand, is the amount needed to compensate the individual who refrains from buying the good at the lower price, or the maximum amount that the individual is willing to pay to be exempted from the higher price and remain at the postprice change real income level. The area P_1dbP_2 is the amount of money needed to compensate the individual who refrains from buying the good at the lower price so that he or she will not be worse off. The individual agrees to forgo the opportunity of buying the good at the lower price P_2 as long as he or she receives a sum of money that would keep him or her as well off as after the price change. EV, in the case of a price increase, becomes P_1acP_2, indicating the maximum amount that the individual will be willing to pay to be exempted from the higher price P_1.

Both the EV and the CV measure play an important role in estimating the gains and losses from proposed projects. They are simply measures of an individual's *willingness to pay* for a change (WTP) or *willingness to accept* a change (WTA). When there is a price decrease (or any welfare-improving change), EV represents one's willingness to accept an amount of income in lieu of the price change or welfare improvement. CV, on the other hand, represents the amount that the individual is willing to pay to have the lower price or the improved welfare.

When there is a price increase or welfare loss, EV becomes a measure of WTP, indicating the amount that the individual is willing to pay to be exempted from the change. In this case, CV represents the amount that the individual is willing to accept to go along with the change. Thus, for a welfare gain measure, we could either use EV (WTA) or CV (WTP), and for a welfare loss, we could use either EV (WTP) or CV (WTA).[3]

Which one is a better measure to use? As Varian (1992) states, the appropriate measure will depend on the nature of the welfare change sought. CV will be appropriate if the desired measure of compensation is more applicable at the new prices (that is, the prices that will exist after the welfare change). For a reasonable WTP measure, however, he suggests EV for two reasons: (a) The measure of welfare change is at the initial (current) prices, and that makes it easier for policymakers "to judge the value of a dollar at current prices than at some hypothetical prices" (p. 162); and (b) the initial prices do not change; therefore, "equivalent variation is more suitable for comparisons among a variety of projects" (p. 162).

On this last point, Freeman (1993) is also affirmative. In a lengthy discussion of the criteria used to determine which measure is appropriate, Freeman explains why the EV measure is superior when more than one policy alternative is under consideration. CV provides different rankings for two proposals to which the individual may be indifferent, whereas EV consistently provides the same ranking for two alternative proposals.[4]

In determining the appropriateness of either measure, Freeman also points out the importance of the legal environment without favoring one measure over the other. For example, in the case of a welfare-improving change, EV assumes that the individual has a right to an improved environment, but CV does not, and that is why the individual will be willing to pay to gain the right. When the change is welfare reducing, then under the EV measure, the individual has an obligation to accept the change and must make a payment to avoid it; under CV, the individual has a right to the initial price and therefore will be willing to accept compensation to agree to the change. Note that almost all authors agree that neither measure does well on practical grounds and that the choice between the two may be based on the nature of the particular policy environment.[5]

Consumer Surplus, EV, and CV Measures

As depicted in Figure 5.3, both CV and EV differ significantly from the consumer surplus measure. Again, the difference is due to real income being held constant in constructing the compensated demand curves. With no real income effect, both curves would coincide with the ordinary demand curve, and all three measures would become identical. As Mishan (1988) notes, "The difference that arises from using constant real income as against constant money income, in the statistical derivation of a demand curve for a single good, is likely to be too slight relative to the usual order of statistical error to make the distinction significant in any cost-benefit study" (p. 29). Willig (1976) also has argued that consumer surplus is a reasonably good approximation of EV and CV, and any error will not be significant given the errors involved in estimating the demand curves.

Although these may not be unreasonable compromises for purposes of empirical research, theoretically, the differences are significant. Such differences, when reflected in cost-benefit calculus, could very well change the outcome of an evaluation.[6]

Nevertheless, despite the differences between EV and CV and the noted limitations of consumer surplus, all three welfare measures are used in cost-benefit studies to formulate, identify, and evaluate possible allocational outcomes.

Examples

Computerizing a Filing System. Consider a project that is designed to computerize the filing system of a local police department. The downward sloping line *DD* in Figure 5.4 depicts the benefits derived from detecting and apprehending violators. As the number of violators apprehended increases, the benefit received from each additional apprehension declines. The cost of detecting and apprehending a violator under the existing program is shown as $0C_1$, and the number of violators apprehended per year is $0V_1$. As drawn, the marginal cost of detection and apprehension equals the average cost, and the time cost and cost of the staff involved in the existing filing system are significant when averaged to the cost of a violator detected and apprehended. The proposed project is expected to produce both significant time savings and an increased number of detections.

Given this information and the use of the consumer surplus idea, we can determine the net benefits of the existing program and show them graphically as the area of triangle C_1Da. Assuming computerization causes costs to decline to $0C_2$ and the number of violators detected and apprehended to increase to $0V_2$, consumer surplus becomes C_2Db.

The net benefit of the project in this example is determined in terms of cost savings estimated as the difference between consumer surplus gains with and without the project. The net benefit is the strip C_1abC_2, which is the difference between C_2Db, consumer surplus with the project, and C_1Da, consumer surplus without the project.

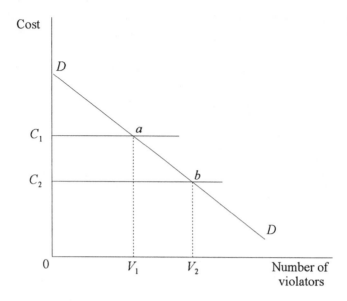

Figure 5.4. Consumer surplus as a benefit measure of a computerized filing system.

Note. The net benefits of the existing program are shown by area C_1Da. With the project, the increase in net benefits is the strip C_1abC_2.

Note that C_1abC_2 is likely to take different values under the compensated measures. Under the CV measure, the maximum amount that the community is willing to pay for the computerized filing system will be smaller than the consumer surplus measure C_1abC_2. Under the EV measure, on the other hand, the minimum compensation that the community will accept in lieu of the project and still enjoy the same level of welfare will be larger than C_1abC_2.

Water Treatment Plant. A city manager in a small town is considering the construction of a water treatment system that will eliminate the need for residents to use water softeners in their homes. In the absence of the project, residents spend P_1 per gallon of water and consume $0X_1$ gallons per month (Figure 5.5). After the project is installed, the cost per gallon is expected to go down to P_2.

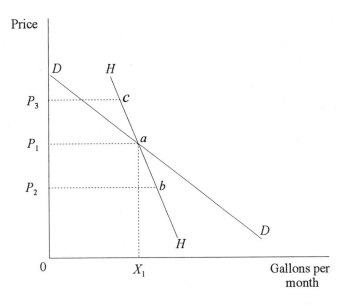

Figure 5.5. Gains and losses from a water treatment project.

Note. Without the project, residents pay P_1 per gallon and consume $0X_1$ gallons. With the project, the cost per gallon is expected to go down to P_2 for the majority of the residents; the maximum amount they are willing to pay for this decline is represented by the CV measure shown as P_1abP_2. For some residents, the cost will go up because of the noise pollution; the amount that these residents will be willing to accept to tolerate the pollution and enjoy the benefits of the project is also a CV measure shown by the area P_1P_3ca.

The results of a survey that the city manager conducts to gauge public support for the project show that most residents are in favor of it, but some are not because of the proximity of their homes to the proposed treatment plant. Assuming that all residents are participating in the financing of the project, it is necessary to consider the evaluation of each resident in the community. First, using the CV measure, we can estimate the benefits to those in favor of the project by simply asking the residents the maximum amount they will be willing to pay to have their monthly water expenditure per gallon reduced from P_1 to P_2. The benefit measure in this case will be P_1abP_2 in Figure 5.5. Second, there may be some residents who are benefiting from the project but, at the same time, find it costly because of the noise pollution from the nearby treatment plant. To account for their share in the benefits, again we use the CV measure, reflecting the sum of money needed by these residents to tolerate the noise pollution and, at the same time, enjoy the benefits of the water treatment system. If their water expenditure per gallon including the external costs rises from P_1 to P_3, then as shown in Figure 5.5, the CV measure will be P_1P_3ca. The relevant welfare measure in this example will differ from its ordinary consumer surplus measure, and the net of the gains and losses to the groups will constitute the benefit of the water treatment system.

PRODUCER SURPLUS

In the preceding examples, the cost of providing an additional unit of the good is assumed constant. Within the relevant output range, the unit cost and marginal cost are the same, and both are equal to the price received at every quantity. Under these assumptions, additional units of output are provided at the same price.

When marginal cost rises as production increases, the supply curve takes its standard shape, which is depicted in Figure 5.6 as an upward sloping line. Marginal cost equals price P_1 at output level Q_1, and when price rises, output rises until MC equals price again. Note that at price P_1, all units within the output range from the origin to Q_1 are supplied at price P_1; therefore, the supplier earns additional sums above the respective marginal cost up to Q_1. This is what economists call producer surplus. Shown by area A in Figure 5.6, producer surplus is the difference between the actual price and the amount that the supplier is willing to accept to provide the good.

When price rises, producer surplus rises; when price falls, producer surplus falls. Suppose price rises to P_2. Because at output level Q_1 the new price exceeds the marginal cost corresponding to Q_1, producers expand output to Q_2, where price once again equals marginal cost. Area C is the change in total variable cost, and area B is the increase in the producer surplus.

Note that the supply curve represents the opportunity cost of supplying an additional unit of output, or if the curve is drawn specifically for a factor of production, it will represent the opportunity cost of employing one more unit of that factor. The opportunity

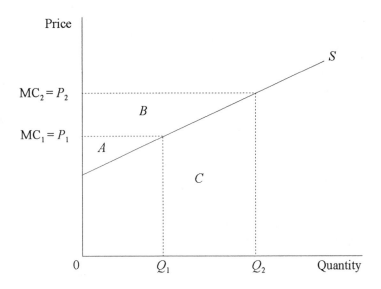

Figure 5.6. Producer surplus.
Note. When price equals P_1, the producer surplus is the area A. It is the difference between the actual price and the amount that the supplier is willing to accept to provide the good. Area C is the change in total variable cost, and area B is the increase in the producer surplus when price increases to P_2.

cost of labor, for example, is the value that labor could generate in its next best use. The cost of employing an attorney in the public sector is what the attorney could earn in the next best alternative employment. Likewise, the cost of appropriating public funds for a revitalization project in a business district is the potential benefit foregone by not using these funds for public education or for the next best public or private project. The producer surplus (also identified as economic rent) in either example is the difference between the market value of the factor and its opportunity cost.[7]

BENEFITS AND COSTS OF A PROJECT

The primary purpose of every project is to raise the level of its direct output. For example, a highway project improves transportation

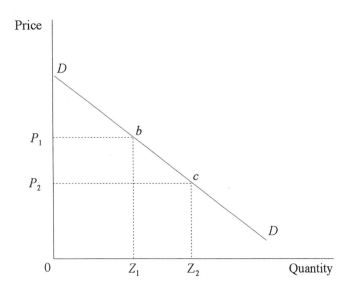

Figure 5.7. Real direct effects of a project—constant costs.

Note. The total benefit of a public project provided at Z_1 is the area $0DbZ_1$; the total cost is $0P_1bZ_1$. If the project lowers the cost from P_1 to P_2, then area P_1bcP_2 becomes the direct measure of project benefits.

efficiency by increasing traffic volume within the projected distance. An agroindustrial project to upgrade processing and packaging quality is likely to increase agricultural revenues in a region. A housing project designed to satisfy residential needs and improve living conditions in a depressed area will probably increase the number of individuals housed among the target population. The intended outcomes in each of these examples are real direct benefits expected from the projects.

   Real effects can be analyzed by using the concept of consumer surplus based on either ordinary demand curves or compensated demand curves.[8] Assuming that there are no market imperfections and that output is produced in a constant cost environment, the *real direct effect* of a project can be illustrated in Figure 5.7 using an ordinary demand curve. The total benefit of a public project provided at Z_1 is the area $0DbZ_1$. With total costs amounting to the rectangle $0P_1bZ_1$, the net benefit generated is shown by the triangle P_1Db.

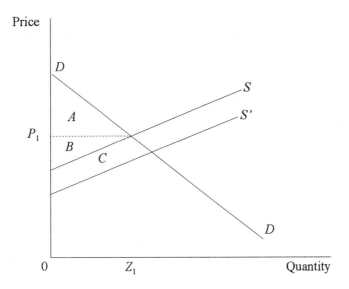

Figure 5.8. Real direct effects of a project—increasing costs.

Note. Area *A* and area *B* represent consumer surplus and producer surplus, respectively. Area *C* is the sum of changes in consumer surplus and producer surplus when a cost-saving project that shifts supply curve *S* to *S'* is implemented.

Alternatively, if a new project is proposed to lower the cost of an existing public program from P_1 to P_2, then area $P_1 bc P_2$ in the figure becomes the measure of project benefits. This is a typical depiction of project benefits under the assumption of constant costs.

Note that when supply is upward sloping (increasing costs), the project benefits consist of both consumer surplus and producer surplus, depicted in Figure 5.8 by area *A* and area *B*, respectively. Thus, in the case of increasing costs, a cost-saving project that shifts supply curve from *S* to *S'* results in increased surplus for both the consumers and the producers. The sum of these changes is depicted in Figure 5.8 as an increase in combined benefits shown by area *C*.

External Effects

In addition to the real direct output effects, the technical external effects of a project must also be considered carefully and distinguished from the pecuniary external effects. *Technical external effects* involve changes in total physical production possibilities in both primary and secondary markets, altering the total welfare of society. *Pecuniary external effects*, on the other hand, result mainly from relative price changes in both factor and commodity markets and involve only redistributive outcomes.

As discussed in Chapter 3, technical externalities are costs or benefits imposed on third parties. For example, in the case of a transportation project, increased traffic volume is likely to cause environmental damage, such as increased noise and air pollution and destruction of wildlife. The external benefit from a new highway might be increased transportation efficiency and its impact on productivity levels in other regions. Building a commuter campus in the center of a city may cause traffic congestion and an increase in the city's crime rate. But external benefits from higher education will also include a more informed and possibly more orderly population, leading to a more intelligently cast vote and perhaps to an overall decline in the crime rate.

Such spillovers, if they have not been internalized by the price mechanism and thus not reflected in the prices of the final output of a project, should be accounted for in a cost-benefit study. Omission of these effects will understate project costs in the case of external costs and understate project benefits in the case of external benefits. Consider the case of understating project benefits because of external benefits as depicted in Figure 5.9. D' and D are the demand curves for a new public good with and without external benefits, respectively. If the project is appraised based on its primary demand excluding the external effects (D), then the benefit cost ratio will understate its social profitability, possibly resulting in rejection of the project, which could lead to underutilization of public resources. As shown in the figure, with project costs amounting to $0cc'Q_1$, the benefit-cost ratio will be smaller than one when the external benefits are excluded but greater than one when they are included.

Identifying such spillovers is not an easy task, but their omission could skew the results of a cost-benefit study and therefore lead to serious resource misallocation. To illustrate the external effects, we refer to the consumer surplus measure as depicted in Figure 5.10. Assuming a constant cost industry case, the initial output without

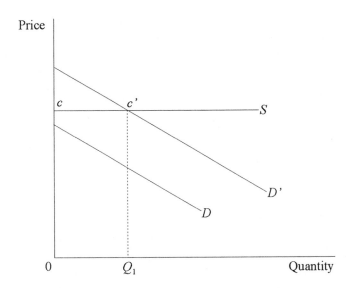

Figure 5.9. Understatement of project benefits because of external benefits.

Note. D' and D are demand curves for a public good with and without external benefits. If the project is appraised based on D, then the benefit cost ratio will understate the social profitability of the project, resulting in its rejection.

the project is Q_1, as determined by the intersection of the horizontal supply curve (S) and the demand curve without the external benefits (D). Now, suppose a project shifts the supply curve downward to S', generating cost savings and additional surplus at the new lower market price P_2. The strip P_1abP_2 represents the primary benefits of the project, and the parallelogram $abcd$ shows the additional external benefits to be realized because of the project. To determine the social profitability of this project, both areas must be estimated and included in the analysis.

Pecuniary Effects. Note that real external effects should not be confused with pecuniary external effects. Pecuniary external effects, also referred to as secondary effects, are gains and losses to producers who either employ or produce inputs and outputs that are identical or closely related to those used or produced by the project under consideration. For example, the implementation of a project may

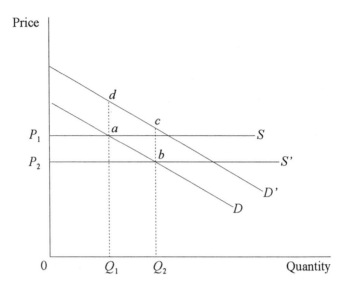

Figure 5.10. External benefits realized from a public project.

Note. Costs are constant; initial output without the project is at Q_1. The project shifts the supply curve downward, resulting in a lower price P_2. The strip P_1abP_2 represents the primary benefits of the project, and the area $abcd$ shows the additional external benefits to be realized because of the project.

result in an increase in the price of an input that the project uses, a decrease in the price of the project output, a reduction in the price of substitute goods, and/or an increase in the price of complementary goods. As the competitive market moves to a new equilibrium, each one of these outcomes is likely to generate gains and losses in related industries (McKean 1958, 136-50). When all such gains and losses are considered, the net change in welfare could turn out to be zero, or the change may be so significant that it could make a difference in project ranking. Should these and all other likely spillovers in both backwardly and inwardly linked industries be considered in cost-benefit comparisons?

Before providing a definitive answer, consider the following examples. Increased traffic volume generated by a highway project is likely to produce spillover effects by changing the sales volume of auto-related goods, such as oil, gas, parts, and tires; increasing the demand for construction workers and materials; and possibly diverting traffic and roadside business from other highways in the vicinity. In the case of an agroindustrial project, industries supplying equipment and raw materials for the project will flourish, and investment in the infrastructure of the area will increase. A public housing project will also produce secondary effects in an area by increasing public health services for the elderly and needy and increasing the demand for construction materials. Are these legitimate secondary benefits that need to be added to the primary benefits, or should they be excluded from cost-benefit comparisons?

The consensus in the literature is that they should be avoided.[9] As already stated, such effects result mainly from relative price changes in private markets and involve only redistributive effects. There may be no net social gains when all secondary losses and gains from a project are combined. A flow of secondary gains stemming from a project might be offset by a flow of losses elsewhere in the economy. For example, the increased sales and earnings in the computer industry resulting from a reorganization project that uses a computerized system will be offset by reduced salaries for noncomputer clerical workers and earnings in the substitute industries. So, to avoid double counting, these effects must be excluded from cost-benefit computations.

Even when the flow of gains exceeds the flow of losses, which is likely to be the case in a growing economy, the difference should not enter into cost-benefit comparisons. Again, the consensus view is that the price mechanism in a properly functioning market will take care of such additional benefits. In a competitive environment, because the demand for the project-related goods will be derived from the demand conditions existing in both primary and secondary markets, their prices will probably reflect all likely secondary effects on these markets as well. However, if there is no market for the project output, then the analyst may assess a value for it and make sure that double counting is avoided. For example, increased wages and salaries of drug enforcement personnel are a transfer of the surplus generated by a drug control project and therefore should not be added to the total benefit expected from this project. As another example, the increased profits of roadside restaurants along a newly built highway are a transfer of consumer surplus generated from the highway that should have been included at the time the project was under evaluation.

In both examples, the surplus generated is estimated by the analyst, and all related secondary benefits should be part of the estimate.

Nevertheless, secondary effects need to be studied carefully because the decision of whether to include them in the analysis depends on the nature of the specific economic environment where the project is under consideration.[10] For example, if such effects represent repercussions on the profitability of the proposed project, then they must be considered (McKean 1958, 141-3). Also, if the profits of the producers displaced by a project cannot be recovered because of the fact that they may be nontransferable (that is, no offsetting gains in consumer or producer surplus can be created in other markets), then it is reasonable to deduct such losses from the project's benefits. Finally, it should be noted that pecuniary considerations may be significant when the public policy analysis involves distributional questions.

Inside Versus Outside Effects

A project may produce external costs and benefits outside the boundaries of its target area. Such costs and benefits may significantly affect the decision whether to implement the project. For example, consider a project that is introduced to increase the standard of living in a community. If the project has benefits that spill over to the neighboring areas and are already included among the total benefits, then the project is likely to be accepted. But if the project is financed by local resources, it will probably lead to resource drain. Therefore, before comparing the costs and benefits, it is important that we determine the boundaries of the project and identify the costs and benefits accordingly.

This presents a distinct problem in the analysis of development programs. Without clearly distinguishing between inside and outside effects, it may be impossible to determine the feasibility of a project. Will the development grant given to a local community be counted as a cost? What about the subsidized low-cost investment credits received by developing countries from the World Bank and other international institutions? Should they be considered as costs to the recipient country? Where should the limits be drawn in identifying the benefits derived from the uses of these funds?

The answers to these questions will probably depend on the types of strings attached to the credits provided. If a credit is a general purpose type, then the cost of the funds used in a project will be the benefit foregone by not using the funds in the next best use available within the boundaries of the recipient country. If the funds are earmarked, clearly specifying their exact use, then the cost to the recipient will include only the subsidized interest payments. If the boundaries of the evaluation are defined to include the rest of the developing world, then the cost in either case will be defined in terms of the benefits foregone had the funds been used elsewhere in the developing world. Needless to say, the benefit-cost ratios will vary under different assumptions and various constraints associated with the use of funds. In project analysis, these issues must be considered carefully.

SUMMARY

This chapter has provided an analytical framework for formulating, identifying, and evaluating all possible allocational outcomes in public project evaluation. First, it discussed three alternative measures of welfare change: consumer surplus, equivalent variation, and compensating variation. Derived from an ordinary demand curve, consumer surplus measures the maximum gains that an individual can obtain from a product. It can be used conveniently in cost-benefit studies, but because it is derived from an ordinary demand curve, which assumes money income constant, its usefulness has been questioned. Derived by using compensated demand curves, both EV and CV measure an individual's willingness to pay for or accept a welfare change, and they play an important role in estimating the gains and losses from proposed public policy programs. Of the two compensated welfare measures, EV and CV, the former is accepted to be superior, especially in providing consistent project ranking. Yet authors seem to agree that neither measure performs well in practice, and the choice between the two measures may depend on the nature of policy environments.

The chapter has also discussed in detail real direct output effects and technical external effects. Direct effects are the intent of the project and must be carefully identified. External effects that are technical spillovers also need careful analysis. They must be properly identified and accounted for; otherwise, project costs and benefits will be underestimated. Even though they are difficult to identify, approximating values for these effects usually improves the results of a cost-benefit study.

It is also necessary to distinguish between real output effects and pecuniary effects. Real output effects, involving changes in total physical production possibilities, alter the total welfare of society. Pecuniary effects result mainly from price changes in both factor and commodity markets. Involving only redistributive effects, they must be excluded because their inclusion will mean double counting.

The chapter concluded with a brief discussion of the boundaries of the target area and the population that the project is designed to serve. It was shown that it may be necessary to distinguish between inside and outside effects and to identify the costs and benefits accordingly.

APPENDIX:
MEASURES OF UTILITY DIFFERENCES

Utility is the personal satisfaction an individual receives from a good or service. It represents a level of satisfaction known only to the individual, and it cannot be revealed or directly measured by any of the conventional scales, such as those used to measure weight and height.

As a subjective concept, utility can be expressed in ordinal measures. For example, each of the indifference curves illustrated in Figure 5A.1 represents all possible combinations of two commodities among which the individual is indifferent. Every point along an indifference curve yields the same level of satisfaction, and each curve corresponds to a different level of satisfaction: I_2 represents higher satisfaction than I_1, and therefore, point b yields more satisfaction to the individual than point a. Note that in the ordinal utility framework, it can be stated only that the individual is better off on I_2 than I_1; it cannot be stated how much better off. Such comparisons cannot be made with ordinal numbers. Alternative commodity combinations can be ranked only by stating simply that the individual prefers b to a.

Utility differences can be measured in monetary terms, however. Two measures suggested for this purpose are equivalent variation and compensat-

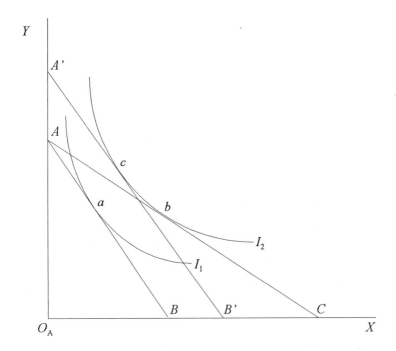

Figure 5A.1. The equivalent variation.

Note. Point a is the utility maximization level with indifference curve I_1 and budget line AB. If the price of X declines, with the new price ratio, the individual can buy more of X with the same income level and the budget line rotates to AC. The new maximization point is b. The individual could have achieved the same level of satisfaction if income had gone up to the extent that it moved the budget line to the tangency point c. The budget line $A'B'$ is drawn at the same price ratio as AB. The vertical distance between AB and $A'B'$ is the measure of equivalent variation (EV).

ing variation.[11] Before providing a formal definition of these two measures, let us first describe what they mean.

The AB line in Figure 5A.1 is the budget line corresponding to a given amount of income and various combinations of X and Y that the individual is capable of buying. For simplicity, Y is assumed to be a composite good that includes all other goods excluding X, and it has a unitary price. The price ratio is the same along the AB line, and given the individual's preferences for both goods, the utility maximization level is the point of tangency between the budget line and the indifference curve I_1. Now, suppose the price of X declines. At the new price ratio, the individual can buy more of X with the same income level, so the budget line rotates to AC. The individual reacts to this change by

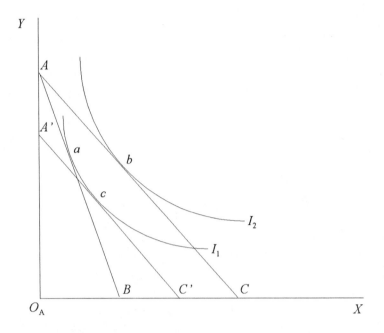

Figure 5A.2. The compensating variation.

Note. The initial budget is represented by line *AC*. A line parallel to *AC* is drawn until it touches the indifference curve I_1 at point *c*. The vertical difference between *AC* and *A'C'* is called the compensating variation (CV). This represents the amount of income that could be taken from the individual while maintaining the same level of satisfaction that the individual had before the price change.

moving to point *b*, where *AC* is tangent to the highest attainable indifference curve, I_2.

Note that the individual could have achieved the same level of satisfaction if income had gone up to the extent that it moves the budget line to the tangency point *c*. The budget line *A'B'*, which is drawn parallel to the initial budget line *AB*, includes this alternative increase in income and represents the initial price ratio before the price of *X* was reduced. The vertical difference between *AB* and *A'B'* in this specific case of a price decrease is the measure of *equivalent variation* (EV). This measure, representing the sum of money that provides the same amount of satisfaction as would the price change, is interpreted as the monetary equivalent of welfare change.

Welfare change also can be measured at the new price ratio represented by line *AC*. As shown in Figure 5A.2, *A'C'*, a line parallel to *AC* is drawn until it touches the initial indifference curve I_1. The vertical distance between AC and $A'C'$ is called the *compensating variation* (CV). This represents the amount of income that could be taken from the individual while maintaining the same level of satisfaction that the individual had before the price change.

NOTES

1. Partial equilibrium analysis focuses on one market. Price effects on other markets are assumed constant. General equilibrium analysis, on the other hand, considers the interrelationship among markets, tracing the effects of changes in demand and supply on other markets.

2. For a detailed discussion of consumer surplus, see Mishan (1988, chaps. 7-9).

3. For further discussion on CV and EV, see the appendix to this chapter.

4. How the CV measure will differ for two different price ratios can be seen clearly in Figure 5A.2 in the appendix to this chapter. For two separate price ratios, the distance between two indifference curves at the initial base price will be the same, but at the new price, it will be different (see Freeman 1993, 57-60). For further discussion and graphical explanation of EV and CV measures, see Mishan (1988, chaps. 59-60).

5. Detailed discussions on this issue can be found in Freeman (1993, chap. 3) and Johansson (1993, chap. 3).

6. For example, in the case of an ordinary demand curve, the problem of path dependency may exist; that is, when the order in which prices are changed results in different amounts of welfare change. If a change in the price of X leads to a change in price of a closely related good Y, the overall change in consumer surplus is A. If the price of Y changes first and is followed by a price change in X, then the change in consumer surplus is B. The path dependency problem exists when A is not equal to B. For CV and EV measures, this is not a problem. For more on this, see Johansson (1993, 38-42).

7. See Mishan (1988, 54-63) for a detailed discussion of producer surplus.

8. For the remainder of this chapter and the following chapter, we will be using ordinary demand curves unless otherwise specified.

9. For a detailed discussion of real versus pecuniary effects, see McKean (1958, chaps. 8-9), Prest and Turvey (1965), Weisbrod (1968a), and Mishan (1988, chap. 12).

10. For example, as discussed in Gramlich (1990), it is important to trace out effects on other markets when "either demander or suppliers have strong cross-substitution effects," and that "there are either nonconstant costs or distortions in the affected markets" (p. 79). Such secondary market effects can be analyzed by use of general equilibrium models, which is beyond the scope of this book. For a discussion of how these models are used in cost-benefit studies, see Gramlich (1990, chap. 5).

11. There are also two other welfare measures that relate to quantity changes rather than price changes. These are equivalent surplus and compensating surplus. As a measure of welfare gain, the former measure is the vertical distance between the two indifference curves at the initial quantity of X, and the latter measure is the vertical distance between the two indifference curves at the new quantity of X. For a discussion of these measures, see Freeman (1993).

DISCUSSION QUESTIONS

1. What are the main differences between ordinary and compensated demand curves?

2. Does the Marshallian demand curve provide a precise measure of consumer surplus? If not, why? What are the other interpretations of a welfare change? Explain how they can be used in cost-benefit analysis.

3. In the case of a price increase, is the CV measure of a welfare change likely to exceed the Marshallian (ordinary demand curve) measure of consumer surplus? Explain.

4. Use the consumer surplus concept to illustrate the effects of a project that is designed to lower the cost of providing good X. Use a diagram to identify the benefits of the project assuming that (a) the marginal cost of supplying the good is constant and (b) the good generates external benefits.

5. Use an example to illustrate the differences between real and pecuniary effects. Is it appropriate to include both effects in the feasibility analysis?

6

Measuring Costs and Benefits

Having identified the costs and benefits applicable to a public project and justified their relevance from society's perspective, the analyst then faces the task of expressing these items in dollar terms to make them comparable. This procedure, which seems straightforward, may become somewhat complicated for the following three reasons. First, price data may not be available for some of the costs and benefits. As pointed out in the preceding chapter, there are some publicly provided goods for which price information may exist, but for most public goods and services, such information is limited. This problem, which arises frequently in valuing such outcomes as environmental hazard, health risk, and loss of life, makes the monetization of costs and benefits rather difficult.

Second, prices may be distorted because of market failures or government distortionary policies, raising the issue of whether they accurately reflect the true scarcity values of resources. Should the analyst use wage rates net of tax or gross of tax in aggregating the total labor costs? What if the majority of workers employed in the project were previously unemployed and collecting unemployment compensation? Should the analyst still use the observed market wage rate to determine the labor cost? Which of the two observed prices, one with tax and the other without tax, is appropriate for building costs and equipment purchases?

Third, even if prices are available and are not distorted, there still may be a problem if the project exerts a nonmarginal impact on demand and supply in related markets. For example, which price is relevant if the market price of tractors rises substantially because of high demand from an agroindustrial project? Should the analyst use the price before the project or after the project? If health care reform creates a high demand for health care professionals, how should the cost of these professionals be treated?

In these and many other situations, it may be necessary to generate pricing measures if they are not available or to adjust those prices that are available but distorted so that they reflect the true resource values. Methods of valuing goods for which market prices are not available are discussed in the next chapter; this chapter focuses on alternative procedures developed in the cost-benefit literature to quantify goods and services for which market prices do exist. It describes those circumstances in which observed market prices are appropriate and those in which market prices need to be adjusted.

THE ANALYTICS OF THE FIRST- AND SECOND-BEST ENVIRONMENT

To trace the logic of price determination in a real-world context and to make price adjustments for possible market distortions, we begin with the diagrammatic description used in the cost-benefit literature. For simplicity, consider an economy with no market imperfections: (a) Individuals are adequately informed of all possible allocation options, (b) property rights are clearly defined, and (c) institutional design is pursued to a level of perfection that is consistent with a purely competitive market.

A society that is characterized by these conditions is depicted in Figure 6.1 by the first-best (grand) utility frontier $U_F U_F$. As described in Chapter 2, the *grand utility frontier* represents alternative points of Pareto-optimal allocations that simultaneously satisfy efficiency conditions in production and in consumption. The most preferred Pareto-optimal allocation is attained at only one point: at the highest possi-

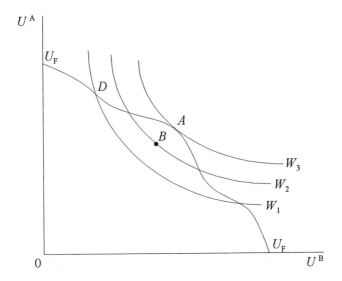

Figure 6.1. First- and second-best allocations.
Note. Point A represents the first-best market environment. Point B is the second-best allocation that is the result of government's distortionary policy.

ble social welfare level. This corresponds to the first-best market environment and is shown by point A in Figure 6.1.

Note that society will remain at the first-best frontier as long as the degree of government involvement is consistent with the traditional principle of tax neutrality. This implies that both efficiency and distributional adjustments are made by a set of nondistortionary policy tools. When society is off the utility frontier, government is able to search for a desirable equilibrium on the frontier by using first-best types of taxes and subsidies.

However, if government lacks first-best policy tools or happens to view distortionary policies as more practical, then the first-best policy environment becomes second best.[1] By using distortionary taxes or subsidies, government forces a Pareto-optimal allocation off the utility frontier, and as shown in Figure 6.1, places the economy at the highest possible level of welfare B, which is inferior to A with respect to economic efficiency.[2]

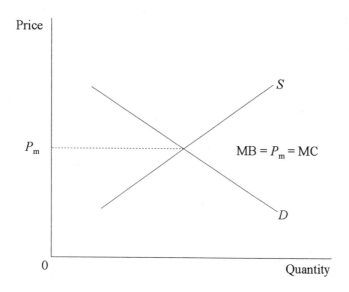

Figure 6.2. Measurement in the first-best setting.

Note. Market price P_m coincides with production (MC) and consumption (MB) values. P_m in this setting serves as an efficiency measure.

Measurement in a First-Best World

Measurement in a first-best environment can be demonstrated in a traditional one-commodity, demand-and-supply framework. As Figure 6.2 illustrates, the marginal cost MC (the production cost of supplying an additional unit) equals its consumption value MB at the equilibrium market price P_m. At this price, society maintains resource allocation that satisfies the allocative efficiency condition of Pareto optimality. Hence, when society considers a new project and plans to implement it within a first-best policy environment, the observed market price becomes a relevant efficiency measure.

The observed market price in this context serves as a precise measure of an incremental increase in society's income and measures the social value of any marginal change in project-related goods, whether such a change results from additional utilization of project inputs or increased production of new outputs. In either case, using the market price as an efficiency measure and retaining first-best

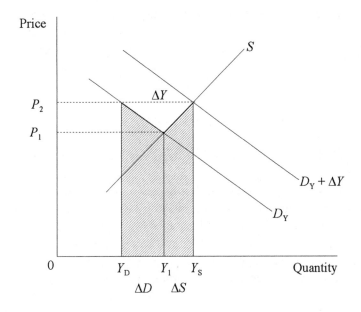

Figure 6.3. Value of a nonmarginal change in project-related goods.

Note. Demand for a project input shifts outward after the project is introduced. The quantity of input needed by the project is obtained by increasing production by ΔS and reducing its current use in the economy by ΔD. The shaded area is the true social cost of using this input in the proposed project.

policy assumptions in financing and implementing a project are appropriate and will remain so as long as the market continues to function in a competitive environment.

Note that in evaluating nonmarginal project effects, market prices may need to be adjusted even in the first-best environment. As shown in Figure 6.3, demand for a project input (D_Y) shifts to the right after the project is introduced. The new price is P_2 and the amount demanded by the project ΔY is the horizontal distance between the two demand curves. If the price had remained at P_1 (that is, if the supply curve were horizontal), then the cost of the input to the project would have been measured by $P_1\Delta Y$. But because the demand curve shifts along an upward-sloping supply curve, the true social cost of the input is measured by price averages weighted by changes in both demand and supply margins. As depicted in Figure 6.3, the price increase caused the production of the input to increase from Y_1 to Y_S and the preproject utilization level of the input, Y_1, to decline to Y_D. Thus, the amount of the input needed by the project is obtained by increasing production by ΔS and reducing its consumption or current use in the private sector by ΔD. Because

$$\Delta Y = \Delta D + \Delta S, \qquad (6.1)$$

the shaded area shown in the figure is the true social cost of using this input in the proposed project.

It is worth noting, however, that because of price and trade distortions found in real-world economies, first-best analysis is rarely used. Yet as a theoretical aid, first-best analysis always serves a useful purpose in determining the relevance and direction of price adjustments in real-world applications. In particular, it forms the logical basis for designing second-best models in a real-world context.

Measurement in a Second-Best World

Market prices in an imperfect market environment usually fail to register the actual scarcity values of society's resources. When society's output is constrained by price-fixing practices or allocated on the basis of false signals, mostly because of ambiguous property rights or distortionary taxes, market prices misrepresent efficiency values. For example, as shown in Figure 6.4, a distortionary tax t on the supplier of Y will cause prices to vary from those that existed prior to the tax. The supply curve S, before the tax, indicates the quantities of Y that the supplier is willing to produce at alternative market prices. After the tax, S shifts to S_t, representing supply prices inclusive of the tax at each quantity supplied. At the point of equilibrium Y_1, the consumption price $P_1 + t$ exceeds production costs P_1 by a distance ab, an amount equal to the tax levied. Because of this distortion, the value of consumption measured in consumer prices will exceed its equivalent measured in production costs. Therefore, an incremental increase in the net income measured in market prices will differ from the incremental change measured in production costs.

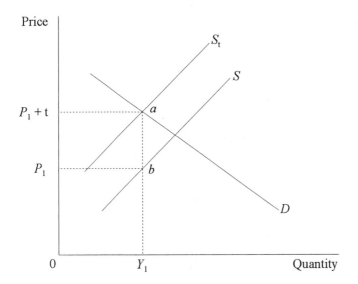

Figure 6.4. A distortionary tax on the production of good Y.

Note. S_t and S represent the supply curve with and without a distortionary tax, respectively. At Y_1, the consumption price $P_1 + t$ exceeds the production price P_1 by a distance ab.

From this discussion, it is clear that under distortionary conditions, market prices are not exact in measuring efficiency values for project costs and benefits. To account for such distortions and to calculate the adjusted or so-called *shadow prices*, it will be necessary to pinpoint the source of distortions and show how they can affect the efficiency values of society's resources when new projects are introduced.[3]

Let us proceed with the distortionary tax example to show how shadow prices are derived. Consider an increase in demand for Y because of the introduction of a new project (Figure 6.5). The demand for Y shifts to the right by an amount ΔY, raising the tax-inclusive price from $P_1 + t$ to $P_2 + t$. At the new equilibrium price, the quantities of Y both supplied and demanded differ from those prior to the project's introduction: the quantity of Y supplied increases by ΔS and the quantity demanded decreases by ΔD. This means that the amount of Y required by the project is obtained from increased production of Y and decreased use of Y elsewhere in the economy. Therefore, an

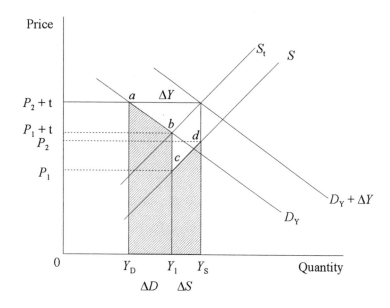

Figure 6.5. Derivation of a shadow price for good Y.

Note. P_1 and P_2 are production prices before and after the increase in demand. $P_1 + t$ and $P_2 + t$ are consumption prices. $P_2 + t$ is greater than its shadow price equivalent, which measures the opportunity cost of Y employed in the project. The shaded area is the shadow price of Y.

incremental change in the availability of Y because of its employment in the proposed project will cost society a dollar amount equal to the sum of the areas $Y_D ab Y_1$ and $Y_1 cd Y_S$. The shadow price of Y, then, is the average of producer and consumer prices weighted by the proportion of ΔY that is obtained at the expense of reduced consumption or increased production. Symbolically, this is shown as

$$P^* = P_p \Delta S / \Delta Y + P_c \Delta D / \Delta Y \qquad (6.2)$$

where P^* is the shadow price, P_p is the production price, and P_c is the market price that corresponds to the production price inclusive of tax.

Note that in Figure 6.5, P_1 and P_2 represent the production price P_p before and after the increase in demand. $P_1 + t$ and $P_2 + t$ are consumption prices P_c (which are also production prices inclusive of tax before and after the demand change). As depicted in the figure, the consumption price (the observed market price $P_2 + t$ after the increase in demand) is greater than its shadow price equivalent, which measures the opportunity cost of employing Y in the project. This is because ΔY is partly fulfilled by increasing Y's production. If ΔY were obtained entirely by increasing the production of Y, then the shadow price would have been equal to its production cost. At the other extreme, if ΔY were obtained completely at the expense of reduced consumption of Y elsewhere in the economy, then the shadow price would have equaled the observed market price. It is necessary to identify the main sources from which the project inputs are obtained in either case and determine the allocational impact that they create in the rest of the economy.[4]

VALUES OF FACTORS OF PRODUCTION

Using a similar rationale, the opportunity cost of employing factors of production in a new project can be determined from Equation 6.2. The opportunity cost of a factor is the loss of output in the sector from which it is withdrawn. Under competitive market conditions, this will equal the value of the marginal product of the factor (the value of the factor's marginal contribution to total output) plus additional costs involved in transferring its use from the initial source of employment to its proposed use in a project. The cost can also be determined from the factor's production function, especially when the factor of production is newly produced rather than withdrawn from other uses. In either case, the analyst needs to identify the net overall output effects of the withdrawn factor.

The Cost of Labor

The cost of a labor input can be expressed in terms of either the value of the marginal product of labor (demand margin) or the worker's subjective value of the marginal product (supply margin) and measured by a market wage rate if the competitive labor market requirements are satisfied. The value of the marginal product of labor

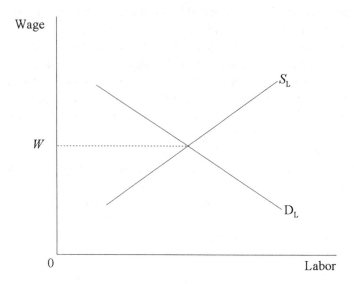

Figure 6.6. Market wage rate under full employment conditions.
Note. D_L represents the quantities of labor demanded at alternative wage rates. S_L shows the quantities of labor that workers are willing to supply at alternative rates. At equilibrium, the value of the marginal product of labor equals the wage rate, which also equals the worker's subjective evaluation of his or her marginal product.

(VMP$_L$) is the value in its current employment of a worker's contribution to the total output. As the number of workers employed increases, VMP$_L$ declines, forming the demand curve for labor, labeled D_L in Figure 6.6.

The downward sloping line D_L reflects the quantities of labor demanded at alternative wage rates. The upward sloping line S_L shows the quantities of labor that workers are willing to supply at alternative wage rates. At equilibrium,

$$VMP_L = W = SVMP_L, \tag{6.3}$$

where W is the market wage rate and SVMP$_L$ is the worker's subjective evaluation of his or her marginal product.

Under full employment conditions, the market wage rate represents the loss of output elsewhere in the economy that results from withdrawing the worker from his or her current employment. There-fore, to calculate the real economic cost of using a worker in a new project, it is sufficient to adjust the market wage rate by including only the relevant relocation costs. Because under full employment conditions

$$W = \Delta Y, \tag{6.4}$$

the shadow wage rate (W^*) becomes

$$W^* = \Delta Y + RC, \tag{6.5}$$

or, alternatively,

$$W^* = W + RC, \tag{6.6}$$

where ΔY is the output lost elsewhere and RC is the cost of relocating the worker.

One exception to the above formulation is that the shadow wage, or the cost of using labor in a project, probably will be less than its market rate equivalent when $W < \Delta Y$ because of the presence of unemployment and/or underemployment. When that is the case, the analyst needs to look at whether society is losing output elsewhere as a result of a new project employing an additional worker. If it is, then the shadow wage rate must be calculated on the basis of both the demand and the supply margins, as described in Equation 6.2.

To illustrate, consider the case of an increase in demand for labor resulting from the implementation of a new project. Assuming that there is some unemployment in society, the hired worker may come from a low-skill, high-unemployment sector or from a high-skill, low-unemployment sector. The shadow wage rate in either case will be a combination of labor demand and supply values weighted by the proportion of those already employed and those unemployed in the total amount of labor hired by the project.

Assuming that there are no other factor market distortions,

$$W^* = W_d \Delta E/\Delta L + W_s \Delta U/\Delta L + RC, \tag{6.7}$$

where ΔL is the amount of labor required for the project, ΔE is the reduction in employment elsewhere as a result of the increase in demand for labor, and ΔU is the increase in the number of workers entering the labor market. W_d is the market wage rate, reflecting the opportunity cost of their foregone use; W_s is the supply price, reflecting the amount of compensation that must be paid to induce workers to enter the labor force; and RC is included to account for the opportunity cost of resources that society employs in placing and training workers.

Note that W_s is subjective, so it is difficult to estimate. As an approximation, the market wage net of tax could be used as a measure because this will be close enough to the amount that is needed to induce involuntarily unemployed workers to enter the labor force. In the case of voluntary unemployment, W_s could be any value between zero and the net of tax wage, because information about workers' attitudes toward leisure and work is unavailable. However, in the case of mild unemployment, it may be sufficient to use the net-of-tax wage to estimate W_s for both voluntarily and involuntarily unemployed workers.

The Cost of Capital

The cost of capital used in a project is the present value of the net benefit stream that the capital could have generated in its next best use. Its value is determined in capital markets where the demand and supply of loanable funds determine a market rate of return r. Under competitive market conditions

$$\text{MRT} = r = \text{MRS}. \tag{6.8}$$

MRT is the marginal rate of transformation, which indicates the rate at which society can switch from present to future consumption, and MRS is the private rate of preference between present and future consumption. The former reflects investment decisions, and the latter represents individual saving preferences.

Because of imperfections in capital markets, the market rate of return could deviate from MRT and MRS. To correct for such distortions, a shadow rate of return is derived. Adjustments are made to account for the divergence between MRT and MRS resulting from distortionary taxation policies and to reflect society's, rather than private individuals', time preferences with respect to present and future consumption. We return to this topic in Chapter 9.

The Value of Land

The value of land to a new project is the net benefit stream that it provides in its current use. If a piece of land that has been considered for a project site is idle and expected to remain unused throughout its lifetime, then its value to the project is zero. If the land is already in use, its employment in a project will cause output loss. For example, the use of agricultural land for industrial purposes will cost society the present value of net returns from the agricultural activity; if the land is idle, the shadow price of land will include only expenses for improving and preparing the land for industrial use, assuming that these cost items are not included among other project costs.

SUMMARY

This chapter introduced two analytical models, the first-best and the second-best environment, which form a logical basis for justifying observed or adjusted (shadow) prices as efficiency measures. Observed market prices in a first-best policy environment serve as efficiency measures; they reflect consumption and production values and at equilibrium represent both the marginal costs and benefits of society's output. However, in a second-best environment, prices lack the precision of an efficiency measure. Generated by a noncompetitive market clearance mechanism, observed prices misrepresent the true scarcity values of resources. If such prices are unadjusted for market failures, they may lead to an unacceptable project ranking on efficiency grounds.

The chapter also showed how to formulate shadow prices for both final goods and factors of production and illustrated how to make the necessary adjustments in both environments when the sources of price distortions are known. Included among the shadow price computations were tangible project goods, land, labor, and cost of capital.

Concluding this chapter, it is important to recognize the limitations of observed market prices. Observed market prices are convenient to use, but it should always be remembered that they serve as accurate measures only under the restrictive competitive conditions of the first-best environment. Under the second-best assumption, they must be adjusted. The general rule in deriving adjusted prices, or shadow prices, is to consider all possible outcomes in the nonproject sector of the economy that may result from employing society's inputs in a new project. This rule is also useful in deriving measures for intangible costs and benefits. Its application to this category, however, requires more effort and creativity. This is what follows next.

NOTES

1. The second-best environment is usually described by a second-best frontier that illustrates the highest possible levels of welfare attainable in the presence of market failures and/or government's distortionary policies. It differs from the first-best frontier in terms of its allocational outcomes, which are restricted by additional constraints imposed in either the economic or policy environment. A market failure, such as the presence of monopoly or government's distortionary taxation policy, could force the economy to its second-best frontier. For a detailed discussion of the first-best and second-best frontiers, see Tresch (1981, 252-9, 296-302).

2. When A is unattainable, society faces a trade-off between attaining efficiency at points such as D and achieving a desired level of income distribution at point B. We return to this issue in Chapter 10.

3. On shadow pricing, see McKean (1968, 33-77) and Drèze and Stern (1990).

4. For more on the derivation of shadow prices, see Gramlich (1990, 60-4) and Boadway and Wildasin (1984, 195-205).

DISCUSSION QUESTIONS

1. Is optimization possible inside the first-best frontier? Explain.

2. Use a traditional one-commodity demand and supply framework to show why market prices may fail to represent the actual scarcity values of society's resources.

3. Briefly describe the conditions under which market prices may fail to reflect the true value of resources used in a project. For each case, graphically show how adjustments are made to arrive at their respective shadow prices.

4. Determine if the following statements are true or false and explain why.

   Under distortionary conditions, market prices are of little use in measuring efficiency values for project costs and benefits.

   In the case of unemployment, it may be sufficient to use the market wage rate to calculate the real economic cost of employing a worker in a new project.

5. Describe carefully the cost of labor under the first- and second-best environment. Is wage adjustment necessary under the first-best analysis? Why?

7

Nonmarket Valuation

Project outcomes such as time and lives saved, air pollution, and endangered species preservation are nonmarket items, and their omission could make a difference in project selection. As noted in the preceding chapter, price-quantity data for the majority of such goods do not exist; therefore, their valuation is often based on information elicited directly through surveys or indirectly from surrogate markets.

The cost-benefit literature provides several direct and indirect approaches to valuation of goods that carry nonmarket characteristics. These include the contingent valuation method, the hedonic pricing method, the travel cost method, and the averting behavior approach. The contingent valuation method is a direct valuation technique that makes use of interviews, questionnaires, and experimental designs to generate data on individual preferences regarding a project outcome or a welfare change. The hedonic pricing method is an indirect approach used to value environmental quality variables that differentiate closely related marketed goods. Another indirect approach, the travel cost method, is applied to evaluation problems linking the cost, total number, and frequency of site visits to changes in environmental quality. With the technique of averting behavior, benefits are estimated indirectly from observed responses to a change in environmental quality.

A growing number of empirical studies and experiments in the areas of environment and health care have been particularly pivotal in improving these approaches and increasing their applicability. A brief review of these studies is provided in Chapter 12, but for a detailed discussion of the methods and a review of empirical findings, readers may refer to Cummings, Cox, and Freeman (1986), Mitchell and Carson (1989), Cropper and Oates (1992), Smith (1993), Johansson (1993), and Hanley and Spash (1993).

This chapter begins with a review of arguments and controversies surrounding the issues of evaluating two particular nonmarket items: time and human life. This is followed by a brief description of the contingent valuation method. An overview of this technique and its limitations is followed by a case study highlighting its application to a specific valuation problem of an environmental good that carries a nonuse characteristic.

VALUE OF LIFE

Placing a value on human life is one of the most difficult and controversial issues in project analysis. How does one compare the net worth of two competing projects, one designed to raise the life expectancy of a middle-aged adult and another to reduce the infant mortality rate in a region? How would one compare the benefit-cost ratio of a transportation project designed to reduce the traffic fatality rate to that of a training project intended to raise the productivity level of air traffic controllers? Should a mandatory HIV testing policy for health care workers be implemented?

Such issues relating to loss of human life or safety effects in general may be overlooked by the analyst. Alternatively, they may be addressed by relying on informal judgment, or more appropriately, conventional economic analysis.[1] One approach that uses economic analysis treats the value of life purely in terms of foregone output measured as the present value of an individual's lifetime gross earnings. Sometimes, however, the foregone output is defined in terms of net earnings, making an allowance for the individual's lifetime consumption. Although such definitions are sound in terms of economic reasoning, they are less useful when individual subjective evaluations weigh heavily.

In another approach, Mishan (1971) defines the value of life by referring to the Pareto principle. Accordingly, the worth of an individual's life is viewed as the minimum sum of compensation necessary to offset the individual's involuntary exposure to an increased probability of death. To offset the increased risk of death, the compensation incorporates payments to the individual with payments to others who may be affected.

Mishan emphasizes that using the Pareto treatment to place a value on human life is not an alternative to other approaches. "It is the only economically justifiable concept," he states. "And this assertion does not rest on any novel ethical premise. It follows as a matter of consistency in the application of the Pareto principle in cost-benefit calculations" (p. 704).

In another study, which deals with the task of assigning a value to life saving, Schelling (1968) points to the importance of the individual's evaluation of an increased chance of survival. A common way to place a value on life is to determine the dollar amount that an individual would be willing to pay to reduce the probability of his or her death. Schelling argues that one way to do this is to use intensive interview techniques.

Note that Mishan and Schelling do not attempt to measure the value of life when risk is traced to specific individuals. When certain death is viewed by an individual, it is highly probable that the value of his life becomes infinitely large. Viewed from this perspective, it seems almost impossible to operationalize the Pareto principle to set a value on an individual's life. (For more on this, see Broome 1978.)

However, projects with varying degrees of risk involving loss of life do exist, and to apply cost-benefit calculus to such projects, some measure, no matter how rough it may be, would seem appropriate. It is important, however, that such rough measures be supported by economic reasoning. As pointed out by Mishan, "In view of the existing quantomania, one may be forgiven for asserting that there is more to be said for rough estimates of the precise concept than precise estimates of economically irrelevant concepts" (p. 705).

Statistical Life

A precise concept for measurement purposes is the concept of *statistical life.* By identifying safety improvements with statistical lives saved, it is possible to adopt measures of willingness to pay for additional safety and willingness to accept additional risk.

Most real-world applications are based on the view of this statistical concept. Jones-Lee (1994), known for his pioneering work in this area, classifies these applications into two categories, referred as the revealed-preference approach and the questionnaire approach. The revealed-preference approach derives estimates from actual choices made in labor markets and from various consumption decisions made against risk of death. Wage premiums paid for accepting risk and all types of consumer spending for gaining safety, such as the use of safety belts, choice of transportation mode, maintaining safe housing, and so on are some of the revealed preferences from which statistical life estimates are derived. The questionnaire method is used to investigate individual tendency toward risk taking under different hypothetical situations. It has the advantage of identifying individual inclinations toward risk of death under a controlled environment, with inferences drawn for different income groups and age groups. Surveying various studies conducted in both categories, Jones-Lee concludes that "neither approach is inherently superior and, indeed, they are almost certainly best viewed as essentially complementary rather than competing estimation procedures" (p. 307).

VALUE OF TIME

In a competitive market environment, the value of a unit of time can be approximated by hourly market wages.[2] Considering that individuals choose between work and leisure on the basis of benefits that they receive from each additional unit of time devoted to each activity, and assuming that the market hourly wage forms a basis for such comparisons, it is reasonable to use the market wage rate to value time. At the margin, individuals compare the monetary return from an additional unit of work time to the subjective benefits that they expect from pursuing an additional unit of leisure time.

Assuming that the marginal disutility of work has already been internalized in the determination of market wages, this rationalization can be expressed as

$$SVMP_w = W = MB_l, \qquad\qquad (7.1)$$

where $SVMP_w$ is the individual's subjective evaluation of an additional hour of work, W is the market wage rate, and MB_l is the subjective marginal benefit that an individual derives from an additional hour of leisure. From this relationship, then, it follows that the time value of a project outcome that consists of time savings either at work or for leisure could be measured in reference to market hourly wages.[3]

Equation 7.1 may not hold in a second-best market environment, however. First, the market wage rate may not equal the value of the marginal product of labor, and the shadow wage rate discussed in Chapter 6 may have to be used to calculate the value of time saved at work instead. A second problem is that time may not be homogeneous. A unit of time may be valued by an individual differently at different times in a workday, just as the time value of an activity may be different for each individual.

Another complex problem arises when it is not clear if time savings result from reduced duration of a production process or from more leisure. In most cases, determining the proportions of work and leisure in the total time saved is a laborious task. Because of the heterogeneity of time in terms of both its use and individual preferences, it is possible to derive some approximations only within the limitations of the concerns raised above. As a quick estimate, however, the wage rate gross of tax for time saved at work and the wage rate net of tax for time saved for leisure could be useful. Another approach could be to use empirical estimation: For example, in estimating the difference in money costs of travel time between two transportation modes for the same destination, the difference would be the opportunity cost of travel time to a commuter. Similar comparisons can be made for particular projects involving specific time dimensions.

THE CONTINGENT VALUATION METHOD

The contingent valuation method (CVM) is commonly used when no observable behavior exists to reveal individual preferences for proposed public actions. It consists of survey techniques in which the analyst, by asking willingness to pay or willingness to accept types of questions, collects information on individual preferences regarding a project outcome or a welfare change.

The information can be obtained through open- or closed-ended questions. In the former, the respondents state the maximum amount that they will be willing to pay for an improvement, say, in air quality; alternatively, they may be asked to state the amount that they will be willing to accept as compensation for deterioration of air quality. Closed-ended questions, on the other hand, ask the respondent for yes/no or accept/reject responses. For example, respondents are asked if they would be willing to accept or reject a proposed tax increase under various response alternatives, such as an increase of five percent, ten percent, or more.

A typical survey instrument provides detailed questions stated under various response alternatives contingent upon a hypothetical market environment. It is essential that the hypothetical change is clearly described to the respondents, including explanations of pricing and financing alternatives. After the survey instrument is pretested and then administered, the collected bids are processed to obtain averages and aggregates for both the sample and the total population.[4] The experiment usually ends with a critical examination of the survey instrument in view of the results obtained and problems encountered.

Note that survey results are likely to be biased because of problems inherent in interview and questionnaire techniques.[5] A common problem occurs when respondents understate their true preferences when asked how much they would be willing to pay for a welfare-improving change, or overstate their bid if they are told that they will not be responsible for the financing. A strategic bias in either case will be present, which may force the analyst to introduce hypothetical modifications in the model to detect possible misspecifications and minimize the sources of biased responses.[6] Other problems include the possibility of outlier bids (the presence of a few large bids), reluctance to reveal preferences (refusing to bid if respondents feel responsible for the proposed change), the embedding effect (obtaining roughly similar WTP amounts for varying quantities of a public good), and survey design problems, to name a few.[7]

Nonuse Values

Despite these limitations, CVM has been used increasingly to elicit information on nonuse values, which include existence and option values. The former belongs to the category of environmental resources for which society reveals preferences only for their existence. Individuals benefit from these resources not by deriving any use from them but rather by realizing that they exist. For example, improved air quality is a use value, but endangered species preservation is a nonuse value. In the former case, individuals pay because they want to enjoy clean air, whereas in the latter case, there is no use value: Individuals reveal preferences by stating the amount that they will be willing to pay to secure the existence of endangered species.

Although the contingent valuation method is useful in providing measures of nonuse values, there are several theoretical issues regarding the appropriateness of such measures. For example, referring to a Boyle and Bishop (1987) study that estimated a $12 million annual pure existence value for the striped shiner in Wisconsin, Bishop and Welsh (1992) question if it is viable to undertake a project to prevent the extinction of this unknown species if the costs are less than $12 million. More interesting, would the taxpayers of Wisconsin feel less wealthy annually if this species were to disappear? That is, as Bishop and Welsh question, "would we conclude that Wisconsin citizens have sustained 'damages' of $12 million annually?" (p. 406). Raising other potential conceptual problems, such as the "implausibly large" amounts when the existence values of all natural resources that can be qualified for existence value are added up and the high average values if fewer numbers of such species are left, the authors point out that neither concern is warranted.[8]

The other category of nonuse value allows for the possibility of future use. This is called option price. Individuals reveal their preferences by stating the amount that they are willing to pay to be able to use the preserved resource at a later date. This category of benefits is different than the pure existence or intrinsic value measures; the latter includes only benefits from the knowledge that the environmental resource is available and preserved. In the case of option price, there will be some use in the future, and that makes the measure somewhat ambiguous. As a result of some possible use in the future, the consumer surplus gained will deviate from the option price, and, therefore, the difference may turn out to be positive or negative. The difference between this option price and the resulting expected consumer surplus is termed the option value.

Despite this ambiguity, option price has been used in the literature as a welfare measure and has been estimated directly by applying the contingent valuation approach. The case study in the following section highlights the results of a contingent valuation study estimating an option price for water quality changes.

Case Study: A Contingent Valuation Study for the Monongahela River

Interested in the water quality of the Monongahela River in Pennsylvania, Desvousges, Smith, and Fisher (1987) conducted a survey to elicit option price bids for water quality changes. The survey was conducted among 393 households living in five counties on the Pennsylvania side of the river, and the response rate was seventy-seven percent.

Before eliciting the option price bids for specific water quality levels, the questionnaire introduced the main design of the contingent market. First, it elicited information about recreational use of the river and introduced the hypothetical market scene for the river. Second, the interviewer explained the Resources for the Future Water Quality Ladder, which guided the respondents to relate water quality measures to recreation activities such as boating, swimming, fishing, and so on. Third, based on a visual description of user, option, and existence values, the interviewer captured the respondents' attitudes toward water quality from each value category. Finally, following a very clear description of how the community is paying directly (through higher taxes) and indirectly (through higher prices reflecting companies' clean-up costs) for improvements of the Monongahela's water quality, questions were asked to determine the amount that individuals were willing to pay for different levels of water quality.

The three water quality levels to which individuals were asked to respond were (a) avoiding a decrease in water quality from boatable to unsuitable for any water-related activity, (b) raising the water quality from boatable to a fishable level, and (c) raising the water quality from fishable to a swimmable quality level. The sample was divided into four groups,

Table 7.1 Estimated Option Price for Changes in Water Quality: All Levels

	Sample Mean		
Change in Water Quality	User	Nonuser	Combined
Iterative bidding, $25 starting point	59.5	51.4	54.1
Iterative bidding, $125 starting point	194.4	79.2	117.6
Direct question	98.2	34.5	55.7
Direct question, payment card	117.9	82.8	93.9

Source: Desvousges, Smith, and Fisher (1987).

and each was subjected to an alternative question format. The four alternative formats were iterative bidding with a $25 starting point, iterative bidding with a $125 starting point, direct (open-ended) question without a payment card, and direct question with a payment card. The payment card displayed annual amounts from $0 to $775 in $25 increments.

The results of the survey are tabulated in Table 7.1. The mean for option prices aggregated for all levels is $117.60 annually for a household basing its bid with a $125 starting point. This is followed by a mean of $93.90 per household with the direct questioning/payment card format. The $25 version iterative bidding and direct questioning without the payment card format provided smaller amounts: means of $54.10 and $55.70, respectively.

Desvousges, Smith, and Fisher (1987) conclude their study with two main observations: (a) The question format seems to influence the survey outcome; iterative bidding with a $125 starting point and direct questions with payment cards led to higher prices than did the other two formats. (b) The contingency valuation method appears to perform reasonably well in the Monongahela River case. The experiment confirms the view that "contingent valuation surveys seem capable of providing order-of-magnitude estimates of the benefits realized from enhancing one or more aspects of environmental quality" (p. 265).

SUMMARY

This chapter has discussed the valuation of time and human life and the methods of benefit assessment. The value of a unit of time is approximated by hourly market wages adjusted for likely distortions in the labor market. In the case of valuing human life, three approaches were reviewed: value of life measured by individual's lifetime gross (or net) earnings, value of life as a minimum sum of compensation to offset involuntary exposure to increased probability of death (WTA), and the dollar value that the individual is willing to pay to reduce the probability of death (WTP). The discussion also included real-world estimation procedures, which consist of the revealed preference approach (actual choices made in labor markets) and the questionnaire approach (application of survey techniques to investigate tendency toward risk).

The second part of the chapter highlighted some of the methodologies used to generate data on valuation issues when market data do not exist. Focusing on the contingent valuation methodology, it briefly described the valuation procedure and pointed out some of the problems that may result because of limitations inherent in survey techniques. These include common occurrences of strategic bias, outlier bids, and nonresponse and starting bias problems. Despite these limitations, the method has proven useful in eliciting information on both use and nonuse values.

NOTES

1. In addition to these approaches, policymakers may also try to achieve maximum safety improvement within given budgetary constraints or employ a decision analysis approach. For a discussion of all of these approaches, see Jones-Lee (1994).

2. For references and further reading on issues related to the evaluation of time, see Nelson (1968), Harrison and Quarmby (1972), Mishan (1988, chap. 42), and the MVA Consultancy, Institute for Transport Studies at Leeds University, and Transport Studies Unit at Oxford University (1994).

3. Note that $SVMP_w$ corresponds to worker's subjective evaluation of his marginal product ($SVMP_L$) at a given market wage, and as stated in Chapter 6, it also equals the value of the marginal product of labor, VMP_L, in a first-best economic environment.

4. The contingent valuation methodology involves several steps, including setting up the hypothetical market, obtaining bids, estimating mean willingness to pay or accept measures, estimating bid curves, aggregating the data, and evaluating the study. See Cummings, Brookshire, and Schulze (1986), Freeman (1993), Hanley and Spash (1993, chap. 3), and Mitchell and Carson (1989) for details. Also, for the origins and a brief history of CVM and its relevance to economic theory, see Portney (1994) and Hanemann (1994).

5. For a detailed discussion of biases, see Mitchell and Carson (1989) and recent articles by Boyle et al. (1994) and Cummings, Harrison, and Rutström (1995).

6. For a critical analysis of how individuals respond to contingent valuation questions, see Schkade and Payne (1994), Hanemann (1994), and Diamond and Hausmann (1994).

7. Another problem relates to the credibility of survey responses. Referring to the embedding effect, Diamond and Hausmann (1994) argue that CVM fails the internal consistency test; therefore, it should not be used in damage assessment and cost-benefit studies.

8. For example, as the authors argue, the problem of additivity is not unique to existence values; it could also be an issue in the case of private goods. Also, the issue of high average value is consistent with the public good nature of existence values (Bishop and Welsh 1992).

DISCUSSION QUESTIONS

1. Outline and discuss some of the suggested methods for placing a value on human life. Is it possible to apply the Pareto principle to set a value on one's own life? Discuss.

2. What does the concept of statistical life mean? What are the alternative measures that can be used to quantify this concept?

3. What kind of information must be gathered to place a value on time?

4. Outline and discuss some of the limitations of the contingent valuation methodology.

5. Can the contingent valuation method be used to elicit information on nonuse values? Use an example to discuss some of the issues with regard to the appropriateness of these values.

8

Investment Criteria
and Project Selection

Once the costs and benefits of a project have been identified and properly quantified, the next step in project analysis is to evaluate these costs and benefits in a time dimension. The analysis at this stage is straightforward: An appropriate discount rate is chosen to reduce the future stream of net benefits to a single time dimension. If the discounted value of net benefits exceeds investment costs, then the project is accepted; otherwise, the project is rejected.

There are a variety of perspectives on what constitutes a theoretically appropriate discount rate. A relatively high discount rate may lead to the acceptance of fewer public projects and thus change the composition of public and private sectors in total resource utilization. The order in which projects are ranked also depends on which of the three rules—the net present value, the benefit-cost ratio, or the internal rate of return—is used. In this stage of cost-benefit analysis, then, care must be taken in the choice of both the discount rate and the decision rule for project selection.

This chapter focuses on these decision rules. A discussion of which rule to apply when the methods yield inconsistent project rankings is followed by a brief discussion of project evaluation under risk and uncertainty. Issues surrounding the selection of an appropriate discount rate are presented in the next chapter.

DISCOUNTING NET BENEFITS

To illustrate the mechanics of present-value computation, let us return to the outdoor recreation project introduced in Chapter 4. The example showed how to identify the costs and benefits of improving the uncrowded shore of a small community and converting it into a public beach. Recall that in the preproject situation, it was shown that approximately 6000 individuals benefited annually from the shore and paid a $3 fee to nearby businesses, who provided parking facilities and services for the visitors and made $0.50 profit per individual. After construction of the new facilities, an additional 9000 individuals were expected to benefit from the beach annually, free of charge. The set-up and investment costs of the project were estimated at $150,000 with an expected lifetime of 30 years, and the annual maintenance and operating costs were expected to be $15,000.

To determine the feasibility of the project, the benefits were defined in terms of consumer surplus gains resulting from implementation of the project. As depicted in Figure 8.1, gains in consumer surplus include two components: the rectangle $A+B$ and the triangle C. The rectangle $A+B$ represents the gain in consumer surplus for those visitors who paid $3 before the project and no fee after its implementation. This amounts to $18,000 annually ($3 × 6000). Area C corresponds to the additional stream of benefits generated from the new users equaling $13,500 each year [1/2($3 × 9000)]. Area A represents the losses to nearby private businesses amounting to $3000 per year ($0.50 × 6000). Combining the gains ($A+B$ and C) and subtracting the losses (A) from the total, we obtain consumer surplus gains of $28,500 annually.

The costs and benefits of the project can be presented in the following form:

		Year		
	0	1	2	30
Benefits	—	$28,500	$28,500	$28,500
Costs	$150,000	$15,000	$15,000	$15,000

The initial capital outlay (I_0) is $150,000 in Year 0. A stream of net benefits (NB_n) equal to $13,500 ($28,500 − $15,000) is expected in each of the subsequent 30 years, with an eventual salvage value of zero.

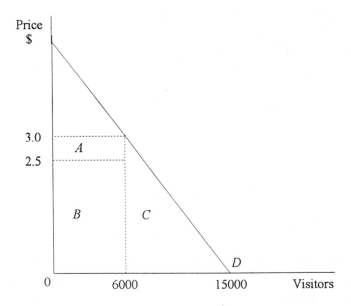

Figure 8.1. Costs and benefits of the proposed public beach project.

Note. Gains in consumer surplus include $A + B$ and C. The area $A + B$ represents the surplus for those visitors who paid \$3 before the project and no fee after the project. Area C represents the additional stream of benefits for the new users, and area A represents the losses to private businesses. Subtracting A from gains yields a consumer surplus of \$28,500 annually.

Next, the future stream of net benefits is discounted to find the net present value (NPV) and calculate a benefit-cost ratio (B/C) for the project. The general formula for calculating the NPV of a future stream of benefits is

$$\text{NPV} = -I_0 + \sum_{n=1}^{N} \frac{NB_n}{(1+r)^n}, \qquad (8.1)$$

where I_0 is the initial investment cost, r is the discount rate, NB_n is the benefit stream that begins at Year 1 ($n = 1$), and N is the project's lifetime. Applying the formula, we obtain

$$\text{NPV} = -\$150,000 + \sum_{n=1}^{30} \frac{\$13,500}{(1+.06)^n}$$

Table 8.1 Discounting the Future Stream of Benefits to Calculate PV, NPV, and *B/C* Ratio

Discount Rate	PV	NPV	B/C
4	$233,442	$83,442	1.556
6	185,825	35,825	1.238
8	151,980	1,980	1.013
8.14	150,000	0	1.000
10	127,263	−22,737	.848

$$= -\$150,000 + \$185,825$$

$$= \$35,825.$$

So, at a six percent discount rate, NPV is $35,825, with a *B/C* ratio of 1.238 (Table 8.1). At an eight percent rate, NPV becomes $1980 and *B/C* decreases to 1.013.

Note that both NPV and *B/C* decline as the discount rate rises. This inverse relationship clearly demonstrates the extent to which the outcome of the evaluation may vary with the discount rate used. Leaving the discussion of discount rates to Chapter 9, we next provide an overview of the most widely used decision rules in CBA.

CHOICE OF A DECISION RULE

There are a variety of decision rules at the analyst's disposal. Although crude measures, such as cut-off period, pay-back period, average rate of return, and so on may be used, there are three rules more commonly employed in CBA.[1] These are (a) the net present value, (b) the benefit-cost ratio, and (c) the internal rate of return.

Net Present Value

As illustrated in the outdoor recreation example, with the NPV method, future benefits and costs are reduced to a single present dollar value. The stream of benefits and costs, either separately or in the form of a net benefits stream, are discounted to find their present value (PV).

The procedure of discounting is straightforward. Using a simple example, if a project yields $10,000 for each of the next four years, then the PV of the benefit stream at a six percent discount rate will be

$$PV = \$10,000/(1 + .06)^1 + \$10,000/(1 + .06)^2 + \$10,000/(1 + .06)^3 \\ + \$10,000/(1 + .06)^4$$

$$= \$9434 + \$8900 + \$8396 + \$7921$$

$$= \$34,651.$$

With an initial project cost of $30,000 and no annual costs, the NPV of the project is $4651.

Using the general formula for calculating the NPV (Equation 8.1), we obtain the same result:

$$NPV = -\$30,000 + \sum_{n=1}^{4} \frac{\$10,000}{(1+.06)^n} = \$4651 .$$

Note that Equation 8.1 is also used when a project incurs annual (recurrent) costs. The annual costs can be discounted separately and subtracted from the PV of the benefit stream, or, alternatively, the net benefits (which is the difference between the annual benefit stream and annual cost stream) can be discounted to find NPV. Either way, the outcome will be the same. To illustrate, suppose in the above example that the project is incurring $1000 annual costs beginning in Year 1. The PV of these costs is $3465, and when the sum of this amount and the initial investment cost ($3465 + $30,000) is deducted from the PV of the benefit stream ($34,651), the NPV will come to $1186. Using the net benefit approach, we arrive at the same figure: Because the annual net benefit is $9000 and the PV of this amount is $31,186, the NPV given the initial investment cost of $30,000 will equal $1186 ($31,186 − $30,000).

Two-Stage Discounting. An alternative PV method involves a two-stage discounting procedure. With this method, (a) the initial capital costs are annualized over the lifetime of a project and added to the annual operating costs to find the total annualized costs; and (b) the total annualized costs are then discounted to find the PV of costs, and that figure is compared to the PV of benefits.

To illustrate, let us compute the annualized capital cost for the above example. At a six percent discount rate, the annualized capital cost for each of the four year-long periods can be found using the following equation:

$$PV = X/(1 + .06)^1 + X/(1 + .06)^2 + X/(1 + .06)^3 + X/(1 + .06)^4 \, ,$$

where PV is the $30,000 and X is the annualized value that needs to be calculated. Another way of stating this equation is that the PV of X dollars of annualized capital cost incurred during the next four years is $30,000. Using a financial calculator, we find X to be approximately equal to $8657.76. Adding this amount to $1000 annual operating costs, we obtain the total annualized cost of $9657.76. The difference between the PV of this total and the PV of the annual benefit of $10,000 at a six percent discount rate is $1186. This is the same as the result obtained using the NPV method above.

This method, which has been recommended by the EPA guidelines, is used to compare annualized costs and annualized benefits of a regulatory option. To annualize the capital costs and discount the net annualized benefits, EPA guidelines use two different discount rates: Capital costs are annualized by using a seven percent private discount rate, and the total annualized costs are discounted by a three percent social discount rate.[2] These rates are discussed in the next chapter.

Benefit-Cost Ratios

Another method closely related to the NPV rule is the profitability index, commonly known as a benefit-cost ratio. A benefit-cost ratio is used to determine the feasibility of a project during any given year or over a time span. It can be calculated by taking either the PV of future benefits over the PV of costs including investment and annual operating costs, or the PV of future net benefits over the one-time investment costs. The former is expressed as

$$B/C = \text{PV of } B_t/\text{PV of } C_t, \tag{8.2}$$

where B_t and C_t are the streams of benefits and costs. The latter is stated as

$$B/C = \text{PV of } NB/I_0, \tag{8.3}$$

where NB is the stream of benefits net of annual operating costs, and I_0 is the one-time investment cost.

Referring to the above example, Equation 8.2 is calculated as

$$B/C = \$34{,}651/\$33{,}465$$

$$= 1.035,$$

and Equation 8.3 is

$$B/C = \$31{,}186/\$30{,}000$$

$$= 1.039.$$

In either case, the project is accepted because the benefit-cost ratio exceeds 1.

Another form, called the net benefit-cost ratio (net B/C), is calculated by dividing the NPV of the project by the PV of costs and then expressing the result as a percentage:

$$\text{net } B/C = NPV/\text{PV of } C. \tag{8.4}$$

Using the same example, Equation 8.4 is calculated as 3.5 percent at a six percent discount rate:

$$\text{net } B/C = \$1{,}186/\$33{,}465$$

$$= 0.035.$$

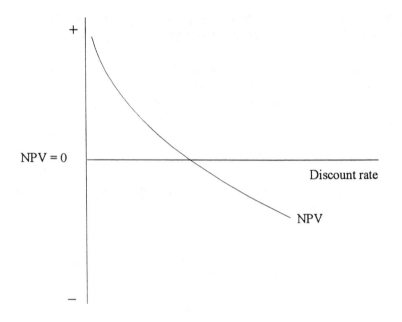

Figure 8.2. NPV at alternative discount rates.

Note. NPV is lower at higher discount rates. At the point where the NPV curve intersects the horizontal axis, the NPV is zero. Internal rate of return (IRR) is the discount rate that results in a zero NPV.

The benefit-cost ratio in this case, showing the income generated as a percentage of costs, exceeds zero; therefore, the project is acceptable.

Note that, as in the case of the NPV method, *B/C* ratios are also sensitive to the discount rate. Both PV and the *B/C* ratios decline as the discount rate rises. This inverse relationship clearly demonstrates the extent to which the outcome of the evaluation may vary with the discount rate used.

Internal Rate of Return

As depicted in Figure 8.2, NPV is lower at higher discount rates. At the point where the downward sloping NPV curve intersects the horizontal axis, NPV is zero. Beyond that point, the NPV of a project becomes negative.

The specific discount rate that results in a zero NPV is known as the internal rate of return (IRR). In the public beach example, NPV becomes zero at 8.14 percent (Table 8.1). This is the discount rate that equates the PV of future net benefits with the initial investment costs. It is calculated by using the following equation:

$$0 = -I_0 + \sum_{n=1}^{N} \frac{NB_n}{(1 + \pi)^n} \tag{8.5}$$

where π is the IRR, and other symbols are defined as above. By this rule, the project is accepted if π exceeds the market rate of return or any other predetermined rate viewed to be acceptable in the public sector. In the public beach example, because the IRR is 8.14 percent, then based on, say, a seven percent market rate of return, the project will be accepted. In fact, the project is acceptable as long as the predetermined, or market, rate is below 8.14 percent.

The IRR method is a convenient decision rule; it provides a quick reference to a project's profitability. But as discussed below, the IRR method may produce more than one rate of return and may sometimes lead to incorrect decisions, particularly in the case of mutually exclusive projects.

The Appropriate Decision Rule

There are ambiguities involved in using the *B/C* and IRR rules. Depending on the procedure used in treating recurrent investment costs, the evaluation may result in different *B/C* ratios. If recurrent costs are included as costs rather than treated as negative benefits, the *B/C* ratio is likely to be different. However, the problem can be avoided if the analyst consistently uses one form of *B/C* ratio with recurrent costs included in the same way they are counted in the NPV computation.

Another problem relates to the IRR rule. When projects are of various sizes, this rule does not provide a reliable basis for comparison. A project with a high IRR may not be superior to one with a low IRR if the former yields net benefits in hundreds of dollars and the latter in thousands of dollars. Also, a project sometimes may have more than one internal rate of return. This happens when its benefit stream is "nonconventional"; that is, in contrast to a well-behaved investment with an initial investment cost and a positive benefit stream, a project's net benefit stream may alternate from positive to negative.[3] When that happens, we obtain multiple rates of return, implying the possibility of more than one discount rate with an NPV of zero, and consequently, the evaluation is inconclusive.

Because of these limitations, the NPV rule seems to be the most reliable. When there are no limitations on the availability of funds, investing in projects with a positive NPV will raise the net return from these projects.

There is one situation, however, where NPV may be misleading, and that is when the budget is limited. Suppose the available budget is $1000, and there are four projects to be considered, each with a different initial investment cost (I_0), NPV, and B/C.

	I_0	NPV	B/C
Project A	$1000	$100	1.10
Project B	500	60	1.12
Project C	400	80	1.20
Project D	100	15	1.15

Project A has the lowest B/C, implying the lowest benefit per dollar invested; but on the basis of the NPV rule, it is the winner because it has the highest NPV. With a limited budget of $1000, we can alternatively maximize the net benefits by either investing in B, C, and D, or, if it is permissible, in two of Project C and two of Project D. Clearly, in this specific example, NPV does not provide the correct ranking.

If the budget had not been limited, that would not have mattered. As long as a project shows positive net benefits, its acceptance would add to society's total return. In this case, all four projects are acceptable because their NPV is greater than zero. Note, however, that if the projects had been mutually exclusive, that is, if we were able to select only one of the four, then the project with the highest net return (Project A) would have been the winner.

In practice, compared to the other two rules, NPV is the preferred decision criterion. OMB recommends NPV as a standard criterion for project selection. However, if possible, analysts are also encouraged

to use other criteria as supplementary information to NPV. IRR computation in particular is recommended when budgets are constrained or
when there is uncertainty about the appropriate discount rate.

RISK AND UNCERTAINTY

The discussion of public project evaluation to this point has ig-
nored the issue of risk and uncertainty. Should this, in fact, be the
case; that is, should a public policy analyst be unconcerned with this
issue? It is quite plausible that limitations of data or uncertainty
regarding the future policy and economic environment may significantly reduce the accuracy of project outcomes. What may seem
infeasible today may turn out to be feasible in the future because of
changes in production technology and priorities of public institutions. A decade ago, very few envisioned today's remarkable developments in information technology, and not many anticipated the
end of the Cold War and the resulting changes in defense spending
projections. Considering that possible changes in technology and
societal priorities alter future costs and benefits, should the analyst
make an allowance for possible variations in the future stream of net
benefits?

Moreover, the analyst makes operational assumptions in estimating
costs and benefits, externalities, discount rates, the project's lifetime,
and so on. Some of these measures lack precision because of the
variety of methods used in their quantification. This is likely to be
the case when the analyst is selecting a discount rate based on
different interpretations and employing alternative concepts of WTP
or WTA as measures of welfare change. How concerned should the
analyst be with such likely ambiguities in project analysis?

One possible answer is simply to ignore the issue of uncertainty. This
may be the preferred approach on practical grounds, especially when
random events seem to be the only source of uncertainty and it is
difficult to assign any meaningful probability to consider their impact
on project outcomes. Or, as Arrow and Lind (1970) would argue, public
policy decisions reflect individual expectations of costs and benefits,
and because the cost of risk per taxpayer is likely to be insignificant,
government should ignore the uncertainty issue entirely.

The opposing view, on the other hand, treats the analysis of risk and uncertainty as an integral part of any cost-benefit study. Given the challenging task of deriving meaningful probabilities for likely outcomes, the analysis is viewed as being useful in providing additional information that could lead to improved project evaluation. The analysis is carried out in a number of ways, ranging from a crude method of cut-off period (undertaking the project if capital costs are recovered within a reasonable period of time) to sophisticated methods employing the theory of choice under uncertainty. The study of these methods is beyond the scope of this chapter. For detailed coverage, the reader is referred to Zerbe and Dively (1994, 301-99) and Mishan (1988, 375-419). For our purposes, however, it is sufficient to highlight sensitivity testing—a procedure most commonly used to integrate risky and uncertain situations in cost-benefit analysis.

In addition to point estimates of benefits, costs, and discounting factors, the analyst may choose to use a testing range for each variable to determine the extent of variations in a project's net benefits. For example, to incorporate risk into a theoretically justifiable discount rate of, say, eight percent, two percentage points may be added and subtracted to calculate the upper and lower bound estimates of net present values. As another example, to account for the ambiguities involved in the measurement of a welfare change, a testing range may be used to show the extent to which the net benefit varies with each of the EV, CV, and ordinary consumer surplus measures.

Quite often, analysts question the assumptions they make because of the uncertainty associated with the parameters they use in their analysis. For example, in the case study of HIV testing of health care workers presented in Chapter 13, Phillips et al. (1994) find the evaluation results highly sensitive to variations in prevalence and transmission risk. In a related study, Holtgrave et al. (1993), as a base case, assumed no increase in unsafe behavior among those who tested HIV-negative. But, because of mixed findings in the literature on this issue, the authors recalculated benefit-cost ratios with increased-risk formulas.

In these and many other real-world evaluation cases, the analyst will conduct sensitivity analysis. Usually, the upper-lower bounds or low-medium-high values are calculated by varying major assumptions based on judgment, literature survey, or assigned probabilities using past data. Regardless of the method used in sensitivity testing, the outcome of the test should be reported and possible areas of improvement pointed out.

SUMMARY

This chapter reviewed the decision rules for project selection. Of the three most commonly used decision rules, NPV, *B/C,* and IRR, NPV is the most preferred. Excluding the possibility of inaccurate project ranking in the case of budget limitations, NPV usually provides a reliable ranking, and therefore it is widely used in practice. *B/C* ratios can be used consistently to rank competing projects only if projects are of equal size in terms of initial capital outlay. IRR, which provides a quick reference to a project's profitability, may not be reliable when projects are of different sizes. In addition, there may be a possibility of more than one IRR leading to inconclusive project ranking. The chapter also discussed the issue of risk and uncertainty. Sensitivity testing was briefly described as a common procedure to integrate risk and uncertainty in cost-benefit analysis.

NOTES

1. A detailed discussion of the crude measures can be found in any textbook on corporate finance. See, for example, Chapter 7 in Ross, Westerfield, and Jordan (1993).
2. For more on the two-stage discounting procedure, see Appendix B in U.S. Environmental Protection Agency (1993).
3. For more on this issue, see Ross, Westerfield, and Jordan (1993, 233-42).

DISCUSSION QUESTIONS

1. What are the three rules on which the decision whether to accept a project depends? What are the limitations of these rules?
2. Which decision rule do you think is most reliable?
3. Suppose a project yields $5000 for the next three years. Annual operating costs amount to $1000 for each year, and the one-time initial investment cost is $8000. Is this project acceptable at a six percent

discount rate? Would you undertake this project if the market rate of return is ten percent?

4. Using the information provided in the preceding question, calculate the internal rate of return and benefit-cost ratios for the project.

5. Consider the following data for Projects A, B, and C:

	I_0	NPV	B/C
Project A	$2000	$200	1.10
Project B	1200	150	1.12
Project C	600	80	1.17

    a. Assuming the available budget is $2000, which project(s) would you consider acceptable?

    b. How would your answer change if the projects are mutually exclusive?

6. Under what circumstances should risk and uncertainty analysis be conducted? What techniques are commonly used in practice?

9

The Choice of Discount Rate

To reduce the future stream of net benefits to a single time dimension, we need to select a discount rate that is appropriate from society's perspective. Is the appropriate discount rate the consumer rate of time preference, reflecting individuals' preferences regarding consumption over different time periods? Or is it the rate of return on private investment (opportunity cost rate) that is likely to be displaced by public projects? Another issue that must be addressed is whose preferences the social discount rate should be reflecting. Market rates reflect the subjective preferences of the present generation and are likely to overlook the preferences of future generations. Should the private rate of time preference be considered adequate enough to account for intergenerational ethical concerns?

In considering each one of these issues, this chapter reviews different perspectives on what constitutes a theoretically acceptable discount rate. It describes alternative procedures used in discounting net benefits and briefly outlines the discounting practices of public sector agencies.[1]

DISCOUNTING IN A FIRST-
AND SECOND-BEST ENVIRONMENT

Within a first-best environment, the distinction between the rate of time preference and opportunity cost rate would not matter because both rates will equal the market rate of interest. But in a second-best environment with distortionary taxation policies, one of the two must be chosen. Before discussing the issues involved in choosing an appropriate rate, it will be useful to define the concepts of cost of capital, rate of return to investment, consumption rate of interest, and market rate of interest.

The *cost of capital* is the present value of a stream of net benefits that one unit of capital could generate in its next best use. This value, reflected in capital input prices in a competitive market setting, is counted as a cost when capital inputs are employed in a new activity. The *rate of return to investment* (i), also referred to as the marginal opportunity cost rate of capital, is the rate at which present consumption is converted into future consumption and is generally based on the marginal pretax rate on investment. The *consumption rate of interest* (q) reflects individuals' rate of time preference between present and future levels of consumption. Referred to as the rate of return on savings, q is the rate on which individuals base their consumption-saving decisions; it is based on either an after-tax consumer rate or a long-term economic growth rate. The *market rate of interest* (r) is determined in the capital market through the interaction of the demand and supply of loanable funds.

Rate of Return in a First-Best Environment

Assuming that the capital market is competitive and remains at equilibrium, r equals both i and q, thus representing both the opportunity cost of capital and individuals' rate of time preference. To illustrate, consider a production possibilities curve that shows alternative combinations of present and future levels of consumption (Figure 9.1). Each point on the curve represents society's ability to convert today's consumption into future consumption. At Point A, for example, society's resources are divided between an amount $0C$ of (present) consumption and an amount $0I$ of investment (future con-

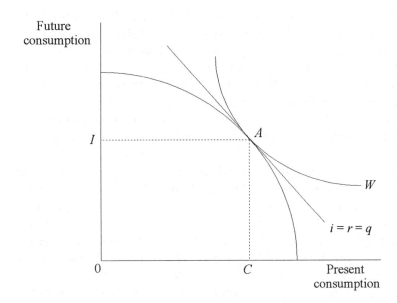

Figure 9.1. The trade-off between present and future consumption.

Note. Points on the production possibilities curve represent society's ability to convert today's consumption into future consumption. Society's preferences are represented by the social indifference curve *W*. The rate at which society is able and willing to switch to future consumption is represented by the slope of the line that is tangent to both curves at point *A*.

sumption). The rate at which resources move from consumption into investment is represented by the slope of the line tangent to the production possibilities curve at Point *A*.

This rate is called the marginal rate of transformation of present consumption into future consumption (MRT). From MRT, the rate of return to investment (i), which represents the marginal opportunity cost rate of capital, is derived. At the point of tangency, MRT = 1 + i; therefore, i = MRT − 1. For example, when society gives up 1 unit of consumption today in return for 1.1 units of consumption tomorrow, MRT equals 1.1, and that means i is ten percent.

Note that the production possibilities curve represents society's ability to convert today's consumption into tomorrow's. As discussed in Chapter 2, it does not reflect society's preferences. It shows the levels of investment that society could possibly make given alternative levels of reduced present consumption. Society's preferences are represented by a social indifference curve (W), and in this case, W represents society's preferences with respect to present and future consumption levels. Unlike an ordinary indifference curve, which describes social preferences for two goods at a given point in time, W reflects society's willingness to trade today's consumption for tomorrow's.

The rate at which society desires to switch to future consumption is called the marginal rate of substitution (MRS) and is represented by the slope of the line tangent to W at Point A. From MRS, we obtain the consumption rate of interest (q), which reflects individuals' rate of time preference (ρ). For example, when MRS equals 1.1, society is willing to give up 1 unit of present consumption for 1.1 units of future consumption. Because at the point of tangency MRS = $1 + q$, q is ten percent.

As depicted in Figure 9.1, the production possibilities curve is tangent to the social indifference curve at Point A. This tangency reflects the equality between MRT and MRS. At the tangency point, MRT – 1 = MRS – 1, and therefore, MRT = MRS. As we have stated, this equality is achieved in a first-best environment by a market rate of interest. In the absence of distortionary taxes,

$$\text{MRT} = r = \text{MRS} \tag{9.1}$$

or,

$$i = r = q, \tag{9.2}$$

where the market rate of return (r) is equal to both the rate of return to investment (i), which reflects the marginal opportunity cost rate of capital, and the consumption rate of interest (q), which reflects individuals' rate of time preference.

Rate of Return in a Second-Best Environment

Problems arise in a second-best environment when MRT $\neq$ MRS, or, alternatively, when i differs from q. As a result of levying a distortionary tax on the supply side of the loanable funds market, for example, the supply of funds shifts up, causing q to fall below i. Consequently, $r = i$ after the tax, with both rates diverging from q.

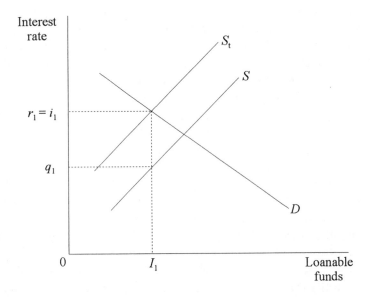

Figure 9.2. The divergence between i and q caused by a distortionary tax levied on savings.

Note. With a distortionary tax levied on savings, the supply curve S moves to S_t by the amount of the tax, and at the new equilibrium, q_1 deviates from both r_1 and i_1.

This divergence is a source of disagreement among public economists. Because investment funds may be raised from increased savings and/or reduced investment elsewhere in the economy, a question arises as to what rate to apply in discounting a benefit stream. For example, as depicted in Figure 9.2, $r_1 = i_1$ and $i_1 > q_1$. Therefore, in the case of increased demand for investment funds, we need to determine which of these rates would be relevant.

To provide an answer, let us examine Figure 9.2 more closely. The downward sloping line D is the demand schedule for loanable funds; it can also be interpreted as an investment demand schedule showing the amount of funds demanded at each rate of return. The upward sloping line S is the supply curve for loanable funds; viewed as a savings schedule, it indicates the amount that individuals would be willing to save at each rate of return. As we already stated, $i = r = q$ in a perfectly competitive capital market. With a distortionary tax levied on savings, however, i deviates from q. The supply curve S moves up to S_t by the amount of the tax, and at the new equilibrium I_1, the market rate of interest takes the value r_1, with q_1 falling below i_1. Thus, the divergence is not only between i_1 and q_1, but it is also between r_1 and q_1. So which one of these rates is appropriate for discounting the future stream of net benefits?

One might choose the rate of return to investment with the view that the return to public projects cannot be lower than the private rate of return. Another choice is to use the consumption rate of interest, implying that the consumer's evaluation should be the main criterion in allocating resources over time. All costs and benefits converge into consumption; therefore, consumers' preferences with regard to consumption-saving decisions should be the determinant. Although this view may sound defensible, the fact that the stream of future consumption benefits generated through investment weighs more heavily than present consumption (i being greater than q) and the possibility that private investment might be crowded out because of public borrowing still may be the reasons for using i as the discount rate. However, the problem is somewhat resolved by the cost of capital approach, which justifies a social discount rate incorporating both i and q. Two alternative methods used to derive such a rate are the weighted average discount rate approach and the shadow price of capital approach.

Weighted Average Discount Rate Approach

The discount rate in this approach is based on the source from which investment funds are withdrawn. For example, when funds are obtained from increased savings, it is theoretically justifiable to use q as a discount rate. If investment is reduced, then i is relevant. If, on the other hand, some portion of funds is obtained from increased savings and the remainder is obtained from reduced investment elsewhere in the private economy, then using a weighted average of q and i will be appropriate.

Consider a situation where the two sources of loanable funds are increased savings and reduced investment elsewhere. Also assume that the tax is levied on the supply side of the loanable funds market. As depicted in Figure 9.3, the demand for loanable funds shifts to the

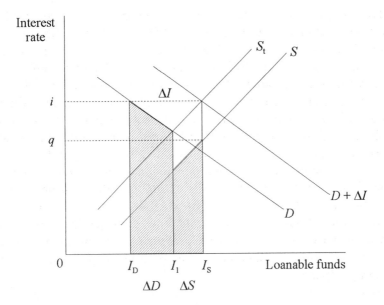

Figure 9.3. An increase in demand for loanable funds.

Note. A project requires ΔI amount of capital outlay. ΔS will be raised by increased savings, and ΔD will be obtained from reduced investment elsewhere in the economy. The shaded area represents the shadow discount rate.

right because of a new project that requires ΔI amount of capital outlay. Consequently, ΔS amount of the required funds will be raised by increased savings, and ΔD amount will be obtained from reduced investment elsewhere in the economy. Shown by the shaded area in Figure 9.3, the relevant discount rate in this case is the sum of q and i weighted by the fraction of ΔI that is obtained at the expense of reduced investment ΔD and increased savings ΔS, respectively. Symbolically, this can be restated as

$$r^* = i(\Delta D/\Delta I) + q(\Delta S/\Delta I) , \qquad (9.3)$$

where r^* is the (shadow) discount rate, i is the investment rate of return, and q is the net rate of return to savers, which also reflects individuals' rate of time preference.

This calculation corresponds to the opportunity cost of public funds view adopted by Harberger (1972). It incorporates both the cost of displaced capital and the value of reduced consumption that is due to increased savings at a higher q. The computation of r^*, therefore, requires information about the relative proportion of displaced consumption and reduced investment elsewhere in the economy, which is rather difficult to obtain in practice. It also provides different rates, each of which corresponds to a type of government borrowing practice and the impact of that on the loanable funds market. If the funds needed for the project crowd out an equal amount of private investment, then r^* will be equal to i, reflecting the value of funds to the private sector. If, on the other hand, the project fully displaces consumption, then the discount rate may be chosen in reference to q, which reflects individuals' time preferences. Of course, there will be several rates if consumption and investment are displaced in varying proportions.

Shadow Price of Capital Approach

An alternate and theoretically more accurate approach to discounting is to convert all future cost and benefit streams into consumption equivalents and discount these streams at the rate of time preference. This approach combines the rate of time preference and the investment rate of return somewhat differently from the weighted average discount rate method. The public project's cost (C) in this approach is the future stream of consumption benefits that would have been expected from a displaced private investment. These benefits, discounted by the rate of time preference (ρ), are then compared to the public project's benefits (B), which are also expressed in consumption values and discounted by ρ.

To trace the logic of this procedure, first take a simple case where ΔI (the total funds for a public project) come from displaced private investment and the entire return to a unit of private investment is allocated to consumption. To find the consumption equivalence of ΔI in this simple case, we calculate an adjustment factor v, which equals i/ρ. The adjustment factor v multiplied by ΔI gives us the shadow price of capital [$\Delta I(v)$ or $\Delta I(i/\rho)$], which is the opportunity cost of the funds invested in the public project expressed in consumption equivalence. The return to the public project (B), also expressed in consumption equivalence, is discounted by ρ and compared to the net present value (NPV) of the cost of the project. Substituting ΔI with C, we obtain

$$NPV = -Cv + B/\rho \qquad (9.4)$$

or,

$$NPV = -C\,(i/\rho) + B/\rho . \qquad (9.5)$$

This is fairly straightforward, and the only difference from the standard discounting is that this procedure combines both i and ρ to find the NPV of a project.

Assume now that only a fraction of i is consumed and that si is invested (s is the portion of investment income reinvested). When only a fraction of i is consumed, a residual that amounts to si accumulates each year. This raises the capital stock by si in Year n, which, in turn, translates into additional consumption. This means that the private investment displaced by public borrowing would have generated income at Year n from which a portion also would have been reinvested, and therefore the stock of capital would have grown because of the reinvestment. To find the shadow price of capital for Year n, income generated from that year's capital plus income from all future reinvestment are converted into consumption and discounted by ρ. The adjustment factor v in this case will be

$$v = (1 - s)i/(\rho - si), \qquad (9.6)$$

where $(1 - s)$ is the fraction of investment income consumed and si, assumed to be less than ρ, is reinvested.[2]

Applying v to the cost of the project, C^*, the shadow price of capital in Year n, becomes $C_n v$. Benefits of the public project, B^*, also can be expressed in consumption equivalent. Assuming that a fraction of public income generated is also reinvested in the private sector, B^* will be expressed as $B_n v$. Therefore, the net benefits of the public project will be the difference between C^* and B^* at each year.

Note that both C^* and B^* will take different values if θ fraction of the funds for the public project displaces private investment and $1 - \theta$ fraction comes from reduced consumption. In this case, C^* and B^* will be stated as $C_n[\theta_c v + (1 - \theta_c)]$ and $B_n[\theta_b v + (1 - \theta_b)]$, respectively.

The NPV of a project, then, can be stated as

$$\text{NPV} = \sum_{n=0}^{N} \frac{B_n^* - C_n^*}{(1 + \rho)^n} \tag{9.7}$$

where N stands for the lifetime of the project.

Social Rate of Time Preference

The perspective of time preference in the preceding analysis can be either subjective (based on the present generation's preferences) or social (adjusted to reflect ethical considerations). According to Robinson (1990), two guiding principles of the subjective time preferences view are,

> First, individuals know best what is good for them, and so subjective time preferences in one year are adequate guides for public investments that will influence utility in future years. Second, only the preferences of current members of society are relevant for public policy; the subjective rate of time preference of the present generation is a valid guide for investments affecting future generations. (p. 259)

The alternate view stresses the importance of the social rate of time preference, SRTP. Time preference, treated at a societal level, accounts for intergenerational equity concerns with the view that government has an obligation to provide for the welfare of unborn generations. A central theme of this approach is that individuals tend to value the present more than the future. Consequently, a market rate reflecting the time preference of the current generation is likely to be higher than the social rate reflecting intergenerational preferences.[3]

There are three specific arguments in favor of SRTP. As outlined by Sen (1982), these are (a) the superresponsibility argument, (b) the dual-role argument, and (c) the isolation argument. According to the superresponsibility argument, government has a responsibility to future generations "over and above the concern for future generations already reflected in the preferences of the present generations" (Sen 1982, 327). The dual-role argument is based on the assumption that individuals as citizens may be more concerned about the well-being of future generations than they are in their role as consumers. In the isolation argument, individuals are assumed to care for future generations, "but may be willing to join in a collective contract of more savings by all, though unwilling to save more in isolation" (p. 328). Because of these and other normative judgments, some authors take the view that the present generation's time preference undervalues public investment and thus may need to be adjusted to incorporate the time preference of future generations.[4]

In real-world applications, such adjustments, which may be particularly important for projects with a long-term horizon, may not be possible, simply because the time preference of unborn generations is not observable. The issue in discounting the future stream of net benefits is to be able to compare the costs and benefits of a project in a single time dimension. Incorporating intergenerational concerns inappropriately could lower society's welfare through misallocation of resources over time. However, one way of getting around this problem may be to refer to government's borrowing rate. As Lind (1990) suggests,

> The government's borrowing rate has some interesting properties. . . . First, as a practical matter it has been in the range of 1-3% in real terms. This makes it roughly the same as long term rate of economic growth. . . . Also, if a country could borrow from abroad, for example, to finance environmental investments, and if the present value of the benefits exceeded the costs, future generations receiving those benefits could use them to retire the accumulated debt plus interest. This does not solve all of the problems, but certainly the government's long term borrowing rate is a good first candidate for the discount rate in long-run intergenerational allocation problems and deserves serious consideration. (p. S-24)

DISCOUNTING IN PRACTICE

From the preceding discussion, it is evident that there is no discount rate that is clearly superior to the others when the economy is in a second-best setting. The shadow price approach has appealing properties theoretically, but the complications and the difficulties involved at the empirical level make the method far from adequate. There remain the problems of estimating the SRTP and/or identifying the relative weights for the two sources of funds used in a project; estimating the marginal rate of return on private capital, consumption rate of interest, consumer's propensity to save, and the rate of reinvestment; and the treatment of the depreciation question.[5]

In practice, it is difficult to make a strong case for or against any rate. All the analyst can do is select a particular discount rate and justify its use. For example, if society's saving rate is relatively low by world standards, then the social rate of time preference probably will be an appropriate reference, especially when the funds needed for a public project come at the expense of reduced consumption. However, if the needed funds crowd out other investment (private or public), then the cost of capital approach (market rate of return adjusted for possible market distortions) or shadow capital approach may be appropriate. Nevertheless, given the current state of empirical studies in this area, it appears that referring to the pretax rate of return to private capital and the federal government's borrowing rates as appropriate discount rates still remains unchallenged.

The current practice in public sector agencies varies. The Office of Management and Budget (OMB) views the shadow price of capital approach as the analytically preferred method for determining the allocational effects of government projects in the private sector. As stated in Circular A-94,

> To use this method, the analyst must be able to compute how the benefits and costs of a program or project affect the allocation of private consumption and investment. OMB concurrence is required if this method is used in place of the base case discount rate. (p. 10)

However, as of today, for most analyses, the base-case discount rate policy designates a real discount rate of seven percent. This rate is justified as an approximation of the marginal pretax rate of return on an average private investment in recent years. Additionally, the treasury's borrowing rates are used as discount rates in cost-effectiveness, lease-purchase, internal government investment, and asset sales analyses. These rates are published annually. For the period March 1994 through February 1995, the rates range from 2.1 percent (three-year) to 2.8 percent (thirty-year).

Two other agencies also use rates on treasury debt. The General Accounting Office (GAO) uses a discount rate based on the interest rate for marketable treasury debt with maturity comparable to the project being evaluated. As an approximation of the weighted average approach, GAO considers its treasury rate approach feasible to implement and relevant to federal financial decision making. The Congressional Budget Office (CBO) also uses a discount rate for most analyses based on the real yield of treasury debt.[6]

Note that compared to the shadow price of capital approach, these rates are theoretically incorrect. However, the relevant issue is to what degree the shadow price approach may improve or weaken the federal government's discounting practices. According to Lyon (1990),

> At this time, the answer appears to be that both outcomes are possible.
> . . . Weakening of federal discounting procedures could occur if the
> shadow price approach is used to manipulate the outcomes of analyses.
> Because the approach yields project-specific results, it is susceptible to
> this danger. Because virtually all of its key parameters are uncertain, it
> is even more susceptible. . . . Despite these cautions, however, it is
> valuable to continue to explore and develop approaches such as the
> shadow price method. It is important for public analyses to be made on
> a theoretically improved basis, if one values a genuine understanding of
> the efficiency, distributional, and other properties of policies. (p. S-45)

At this time, however, as the methods of shadow pricing continue to improve, one practical approach may be to evaluate the present value of a project over a range of discount rates and to determine a reasonably wide sensitivity testing range with selected upper and lower bound discount rates. As Lind (1990) concludes in his examination of discount rate policy, an appropriate discount policy will depend on special circumstances characterizing the policy problem.

SUMMARY

The market rate of interest in a first-best environment equals both the consumption rate of interest and the rate of return to investment.

Therefore, any of the three rates can be used as a discount rate. A problem arises in a second-best environment. In real-world applications, the rate of return to investment may diverge from the consumption rate of interest because of distortionary taxation policies. The issue is to determine what rate to apply in discounting a net benefit stream.

Those who propose the rate of return to investment as a discount rate argue that the return to public projects cannot be lower than the rate of return to a private project. On the other hand, proponents of the consumption rate of interest (reflecting the rate of time preference) argue that the consumer's evaluation should be the main criterion in allocating resources over time.

A compromise approach combines both rates to derive either a weighted average discount rate or the shadow price of capital. The weighted average discount rate is the sum of the consumption rate of interest and the rate of return to investment weighted by the fractions of displaced consumption and reduced investment elsewhere in the economy, respectively. The theoretically more accurate shadow price of capital approach converts all future cost and benefit streams into consumption equivalents and discounts these streams at the rate of time preference.

In practice, the shadow price of capital is the analytically preferred method, but it is difficult to apply. For most analyses involving public sector agencies, the discount rate is seven percent. This rate is justified as an approximation of the marginal pretax rate of return on average investment in a given time period.

NOTES

1. For references and further reading on many issues raised in this chapter, the reader may refer to Feldstein (1964), Gramlich (1990, chap. 6), Harberger (1972), Marglin (1963), Tresch (1981, chap. 24), Lind (1982), and Robinson (1990).

2. As discussed in Chapter 14, v is the social value of savings. When project benefits are measured in consumption, v is applied as a premium on savings. When public income is the unit of account, then v is the social value of public income and is used to discount private consumption. Also, notice that in Equation 9.6, si accounts for the multiplicative effects of additional savings that are assumed to be reinvested, and v will be infinite if $si > \rho$ and si appears in the denominator. For the derivation and detailed discussion of v, see Zerbe and Dively (1994, 282-6).

3. In addition, the evolution of environmental effects may also justify a lower social rate of return over time. As Weitzman argues,

> Essentially, the social rate of return on investment decreases with the level of development because each extra unit of consumption is becoming less valuable relative to the negative externality of increased economic activity required to bring about the extra consumption. Such logic explains why the social or environmental rate of return might be expected to decline over time relative to the private rate of return. (p. 207)

For details, see Weitzman (1994).

4. For more on the individual and societal perspectives of time preferences, see Robinson (1990) and Krahn and Gafni (1993).

5. The treatment of depreciation and the rate of return to investment is very important because they affect the size of the calculated shadow price of capital. The shadow price estimates are very sensitive to the values of these variables. For details, see Table 2 in Lyon (1990); also, see Bradford (1975) and Mendelsohn (1981).

6. For the details of government's discount rate policy, see Hartman (1990), Lyon (1990), Lind (1990), and U.S. General Accounting Office (1992).

DISCUSSION QUESTIONS

1. Compare and contrast the following concepts:

   a. MRT versus MRS
   b. rate of return to investment versus consumption rate of interest
   c. rate of return to investment versus marginal rate of transformation
   d. rate of return to saving versus marginal rate of substitution

2. Use a production possibilities curve and show how MRT may diverge from MRS.

3. Use the loanable funds market diagram and illustrate how a tax on the demand side of the loanable funds market creates distortions.

4. Using the diagram in the preceding question, show how to calculate the cost of capital when there is a nonmarginal increase in the demand for loanable funds.

5. Describe the alternative views of discounting the net benefits of public projects. Which view is more appropriate if society is substantially underinvesting?

6. Outline some of the arguments against using the market rate of return to discount the net benefits in public project evaluation. Would you still recommend the weighted average discount rate approach if the funds are obtained at the expense of reduced investment in the private sector?

10

Income Distribution as
an Evaluation Criterion

The evaluation methodology described so far has used efficiency as the sole criterion in determining the economic feasibility of a public project. Using this standard, a project is acceptable as long as it generates net gains in compliance with the Kaldor-Hicks efficiency criterion. As an alternative to this traditional approach, equity also may be integrated into the analysis. This often requires an evaluation design that identifies the winners and losers of a project and determines if the welfare change is an improvement from society's perspective.

There are three equity related questions that the analyst needs to consider: (a) Should society seek projects that would drive scarce resources toward the first-best welfare (Pareto-optimum) frontier and simply be unconcerned with income redistribution? (b) Should society strive for the first-best frontier initially and then move to a higher social welfare level through income redistribution programs? (c) Should efficiency and equity criteria be considered simultaneously in project evaluation?

The response to the first question is usually affirmative. Viewing resource allocation problems from the perspective of efficiency criteria alone is not only theoretically convenient but also consistent with mainstream economic reasoning. According to this view, increasing the size of the total pie is important, and redistributions that could affect its size adversely should be avoided. Furthermore, because the cost of identifying such effects may be substantial, incorporating them in the analysis may be untenable.

The detachment of efficiency from equity in the second question also provides a convenient conceptualization for the attainment of social welfare maximization. This is a particularly defensible position when income redistribution is viewed as a separate goal that is achievable through nondistortionary taxation and subsidization policies. According to this view, one of government's roles is to guide society toward its welfare frontier and carry out income redistribution with maximum income possible. Yet when projects with negative present values are implemented to satisfy the distributional goal, society moves below its welfare frontier. Assuming that public policies could redistribute income effectively if necessary, with less than efficient income generated from equity-oriented projects, government's redistribution efforts will be affected adversely.[1]

As for the third question, whether to incorporate both efficiency and equity considerations in project evaluation, the decision is a matter of preference. It is fairly common to include both criteria in regional as well as country development studies. That is because projects that may be feasible on efficiency grounds could change income distribution significantly, generating both intratemporal (intragenerational) and intertemporal (intergenerational) distribution problems that cannot be corrected through existing income redistribution programs. Therefore, before proceeding with the selection stage of project evaluation, all project outcomes should be reevaluated in terms of their combined allocational and distributional effects.

This chapter focuses on some of the alternative ways of incorporating both allocational and distributional considerations in project evaluation. The first section briefly reviews two formulations of social welfare functions. The second section discusses the rationale for government's involvement in income redistribution and briefly describes two methods for the derivation of distributional weights.

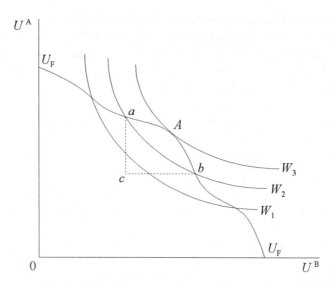

Figure 10.1. Optimal resource allocation in line with society's distributive justice norms.

Note. A movement from c toward any point on the frontier is allocational, and any movement from either a or b toward A is distributional, resulting in optimal resource allocation in line with society's distributional norms.

EFFICIENCY, EQUITY, AND PROJECT EVALUATION

As described in Chapter 2, an infinite number of Pareto-optimal allocations exist, but only one satisfies social welfare maximization conditions. Given society's social welfare function, which represents alternative combinations of individual utility levels among which society is indifferent, the tangency between the grand utility frontier and the highest attainable social welfare curve determines the welfare-maximum allocation. As depicted in Figure 10.1, a movement from point c toward any point on the frontier is allocational, and any movement from either a or b toward the tangency point A is distributional, resulting in optimal resource allocation in line with society's distributive justice norms.

Note that the solution to A requires knowledge of a social welfare function. As we have shown in Chapter 2, the functional form used in

Figure 10.1 allows for an ordinal ranking of social preferences and satisfies the Pareto criterion: if one individual's utility increases while all other utilities are held constant, social welfare must increase.

One formulation of the social welfare function draws on *utilitarianism* and revolves around the principle of maximizing society's total utility. According to this principle, social welfare is the sum of each individual's utility, and redistribution of income is justified as long as it raises total welfare. For example, assuming that individuals have unequal marginal utility schedules, income is redistributed from those with low capacity to enjoy additional income to those with higher capacity to do so. This implies that in a simplified model of two individuals, income will be transferred to the individual who has the higher marginal utility of income, and the transfer will continue until the marginal utility of income for both individuals is equal. It should be noted that this does not lead to absolute income equality. Under utilitarianism, perfect equality of income is possible only if individuals have similar utility functions.

There is also the maximin formulation of the social welfare function, which is based on *Rawlsian distributive justice.* According to Rawls, every distribution should benefit the least advantaged member of society. Individuals have a right to claim basic liberties, and therefore no individual will agree to the risk of being in poverty. This sense of risk induces individuals to accept a level of distribution that would benefit the most disadvantaged members of society.[2]

Each of these welfare functions has important implications in determining an ethical income distribution. A competitive market attains a Pareto-optimal allocation and also achieves a market-determined welfare distribution. If the market-determined distribution fails to conform to society's ethical norms, then some redistribution of income, or wealth, becomes socially desirable. At this point, social welfare functions serve as useful conceptual tools in determining both the principles and the logic of possible distributions.

Income Redistribution and Project Evaluation

As shown in Chapter 2, society tends to move toward a Pareto-optimum and welfare-maximum allocation, assuming that all markets clear and public policies are in line with a first-best policy environment. When

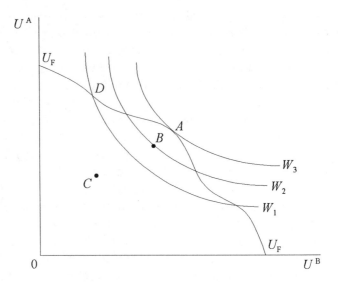

Figure 10.2. Distributional changes resulting from distortionary taxation and expenditure policies.

Note. From C, society moves to D first and adjusts to A using lump-sum distributions. A project that takes society to B is preferred to an alternative project aiming at D. B is superior to D in terms of welfare gains but inferior to A on both efficiency and equity grounds.

the economy is below the efficiency frontier, first-best measures may be employed to bring the economy not just to any point on the frontier but to the point where both Pareto efficiency and a welfare maximum allocation are attained. This means that projects that would move the economy to the frontier are accepted on efficiency grounds, and that the efficient income generated is distributed in line with society's redistribution norms. As shown in Figure 10.2, from an initial point C, society moves to D first and adjusts to A through the use of lump-sum distributions. At D, efficiency is attained, and at A, efficiency is attained and welfare is maximized.

However, this solution may present a serious problem when government chooses to follow distortionary policies. For example, point A may be unattainable because of government's distortionary taxation and expenditure policies, especially if government uses individual income taxes and other forms of personal taxes to alter income distribution. These policies may create price distortions, resulting in additional distributional changes. Thus, from an efficient allocation *D* in Figure 10.2, government may drive the economy to *B* by following distortionary taxation and expenditure policies.

Note that *B* is superior to *D* in terms of welfare gains but inferior to *A* on both efficiency and equity grounds. This presents a crucial decision for the policymaker: choosing between a project to generate maximum income and a project to maximize welfare. For example, from an initial situation *C*, government may either move to point *D* or choose *B* to maximize welfare, causing inefficiency for the sake of equity in a distorted economic and policy environment. A project that takes society to *B* is more preferred than an alternative project aiming at *D*, because the former, despite its lower present value, is superior on the basis of social welfare rankings.[3]

Thus, in this second-best framework, income redistribution becomes an issue. Lacking a first-best policy environment, there will be a basis for equity adjustments, which can be made through a number of social welfare programs at various governmental levels or through public projects adjusted by either aggregate or project-specific distributional weights.

Welfare programs include a wide range of transfer payments, such as grants and many forms of in-kind contributions. These are provided either on an individual basis or per jurisdiction to make adjustments for both interjurisdictional externalities and distributional deficiencies resulting from an inadequate tax base in the recipient communities.

Distributional weights, on the other hand, are used to make distributional adjustments at the project level. They can be derived from either national or project-specific parameters that allow for the consideration of relative preferences attached to different income groups in a society. They also include intertemporal parameters, which weigh society's relative priorities regarding present versus future consumption. In the remainder of the chapter, we show how these weights are calculated and incorporated into project evaluation.

DISTRIBUTIONAL WEIGHTS

Suppose the net benefits of a project are divided between two income groups: the high-income group (*H*) and the low-income group

(L). Assuming that the project has passed the Kaldor-Hicks test, the net benefits (NB) will be stated as

$$NB = w_h\Delta H + w_l\Delta L,\qquad(10.1)$$

where both w_h and w_l equal one. This assumes that the marginal utility of income for both income groups is the same, and therefore no distributional weight assignment is necessary. If NB exceeds zero, the project is accepted.

Note that the marginal utility of income for either group is not known, and in reality, it may differ across income groups. For illustration, suppose the net benefits of a project provide increased income of $300 for H and a loss in income of $100 for L. Applying the Kaldor-Hicks criterion, the net benefit of the project is $200, which is the right amount for the project to pass the test. Assuming marginal utility of income is one for both income groups, the net benefit of $200 will also represent the change in economic welfare.

However, there would be a discrepancy between income and economic welfare generated if the marginal utility of income is, in fact, different for each individual. As indicated, the marginal utility of income is unknown or cannot be measured, but for illustration, suppose it is .40 for H and 1.25 for L. This means that a $1 change in income is equivalent to a $0.40 change in economic welfare for H and a $1.25 change for L.

Applying these weights, the overall change in economic welfare will be

$$NB = (0.40 \times \$300) + (1.25 \times -\$100)$$

$$= \$120 + (-\$125)$$

$$= -\$5.$$

So, with the marginal utility of income unknown, it is possible that a project that is accepted on the Kaldor-Hicks criterion may, in fact, reduce economic welfare.[4]

From the preceding, it is clear that if maximizing welfare is a goal and applying distributional weights is more feasible than using income transfers, in addition to clearly identifying the potential winners and losers of a project, it is also important that the assigned weights reflect the marginal utility of income values of different income groups. Otherwise, projects evaluated on subjective weights could turn out to be nonoptimal, preventing society from achieving both its efficiency and its equity goals.

Derivation of Distributional Weights

Distributional weights are typically calculated relative to a median income. Applying alternative values for the marginal social utility of income parameter, distributional weights can be estimated using a simple formula:

$$d = (y/y_m)^{-\eta} , \qquad (10.2)$$

where η is the marginal social utility of income parameter, y is the income of individuals affected by a project, and y_m is the median income.[5] When $\eta = 0$, $d = 1$. When $\eta = 1$, d takes different values based on y; for example, for $y = \$10,000$ and $y_m = \$15,000$, d equals 1.5.

Distributional weights can be derived based on (a) ex post knowledge of the distributional aspects of already implemented public policies, or (b) distributional considerations implicit in society's aggregate welfare parameters. The best-known model following the first approach was developed by Burton Weisbrod (1968b), and for the second approach, the most complete methodology was developed by the World Bank (see Squire and van der Tak 1975; Ray 1984). A brief review of both methodologies is provided below. For a complete description and the analysis of these methodologies, the reader should refer to the original work.

Weisbrod's Distributional Weights. The distributional weights in Weisbrod's approach are observed values residually derived on the assumption that any observed deviation from efficiency is explained by income distribution considerations. As an example, the model considers a set of projects $(P_1, \ldots P_n)$ with m groups of beneficiaries. In a case of four projects and four groups of beneficiaries, the model assumes that (a) only one project (P_1) is rejected and the other three $(P_2, P_3,$ and $P_4)$

are accepted; (b) the net benefits of the rejected project are higher than those of any of the three accepted projects; and (c) on the efficiency criterion alone, the rejected project would have been acceptable.

Assuming that the distribution of benefits among the beneficiaries is estimated correctly, the model calculates distributional weights (α_1, α_2, α_3, α_4) from a system of equations. These are the weights that would justify the rejection of P_1 and the acceptance of the other three projects.

Note that for the model to provide solutions, the number of equations and the number of projects must be equal, and there should be no doubt about the reasoning behind the selection of less efficient projects. Otherwise, as Tresch (1981) writes,

> Perhaps the weights Weisbrod estimated are plausible, but there is really no reason to believe that the α_i are actually measuring social marginal utilities of income. They could be easily picking up other factors such as intangible costs and benefits, or blatant political partisanship. Unfortunately, Weisbrod's interpretation of the α_i is only as good as his heroic assumptions that government project selection embodies only efficiency and equity criteria, and that it combines them in accordance with the dictates of neoclassical theory. (p. 553)

Another objection is from Layard (1972): "Either the government's decisions so far have been consistent, in which case why worry about helping it continue to be consistent, or they have been inconsistent, in which case why pretend they were consistent" (p. 60).

The World Bank Model. The distributional weights in the World Bank approach are derived from social value parameters that account for both the income distribution effect and the savings effect of a project. These include (a) intratemporal parameters that allow for relative consumption preferences attached to each person or to specific income groups, and (b) intertemporal parameters reflecting society's relative priorities regarding saving versus consumption. These weights are included in the net social benefit computation as follows:

$$\text{NSB} = S + C\,(d/v) \tag{10.3}$$

where NSB is the net social benefit, S is savings, C is consumption, d is the social value of private consumption, and v is the social value of savings (or public income).

The social value of private consumption (d) is the intratemporal parameter that is used to weight the consumption of a specific income group relative to base-level consumption. It is derived using a functional form similar to that of Equation 10.2. Note that in Equation 10.2, d is calculated relative to a median income. In the World Bank methodology, on the other hand, d is calculated relative to a base level of consumption. As described in detail in the appendix to this chapter, the base level of consumption is the level at which private consumption and public income are considered equally valuable on the margin. This is the cut-off level of consumption that is considered as the basis for granting welfare benefits. Because this level of consumption cannot be determined in practice, society's average consumption level is used as a proxy.

The intertemporal parameter (v), which stands for the social value of savings, can be used either as a premium or as a discount factor. When project benefits are measured using consumption as the numeraire, v indicates the social value of private savings and is applied as a premium on savings. However, if public income is the numeraire, then v is treated as the social value of public income and is used for discounting private consumption. This parameter is calculated from the following equation:

$$v = (1 - s)i/(\rho - si) , \qquad (10.4)$$

where $(1 - s)$ is the fraction of income consumed, i is the return to investment, and ρ is the rate of time preference.[6]

To calculate this parameter, suppose the marginal propensity to save (s) is .2, the rate of return to a unit of investment (i) is .18, and the consumption rate of interest (ρ) is .08. Using Equation 10.4, we find $v = 3.27$. This means that a $1 increase in income generated by a project is worth $3.27 of private consumption.

SUMMARY

According to the Kaldor-Hicks criterion, a project is accepted as long as the gains from the project exceed the losses. Should this be the only test for accepting a project, or should the analyst also identify the winners and losers and determine if the change in economic welfare is an improvement from the perspective of the economically disadvantaged? This chapter briefly reviewed the issues surrounding this question. One conclusion consistent with the traditional approach was that income generated from projects implemented on efficiency grounds is best distributed, if necessary, by the government, provided that it uses nondistortionary tax and subsidy measures. Therefore, in this case, the analyst need not be concerned with the equity question. However, in the presence of distortionary government policies, a trade-off exists between efficiency and equity. Government may choose a project to maximize welfare, causing inefficiency for the sake of equity.

Equity adjustments can be made through a variety of social welfare programs. They also can be made through distributional weights derived from either national or project-specific parameters. The chapter concluded with a brief description of two methods to derive distributional weights: one based on information on previously implemented projects and the other based on society's aggregate welfare parameters.

APPENDIX:
DISTRIBUTIONAL WEIGHTS

Income Distribution Effect

The derivation of income-specific distribution weights (d_i) is based on a utility function that assumes diminishing marginal utility. The relevant parameter of the function is the income elasticity of marginal utility, defined as the percentage by which the utility derived from a unit of income varies with changes in income. We can infer from this measure how much the marginal utility of consumption decreases as the level of consumption increases.

The utility function can be stated as

$$\partial U/\partial c_i = c^{-}\eta_i \,, \qquad\qquad (10A.1)$$

where $\partial U/\partial c_i$ is marginal utility at consumption level c_i, and η is the elasticity of marginal utility. The negative sign indicates that η falls as consumption rises, implying a smaller welfare loss from reduced consumption by high-income groups than the loss by low-income groups.

The distributional weights are derived by taking the ratio of marginal utility at a given level of consumption c_i over the base level of consumption c^*. Symbolically, this ratio can be stated as

$$d_i = (\partial U/\partial c_i)/(\partial U/c^*), \qquad (10A.2)$$

which may be expressed as

$$d_i = (c_i/c^*)^{-}\eta \qquad (10A.3)$$

or

$$d_i = (c^*/c_i)\eta. \qquad (10A.4)$$

According to Equation 10A.4, the value of distributional weights depends on the base level of consumption and the elasticity of marginal utility. The base level of consumption c^* is the level at which private consumption and public income are considered equally valuable on the margin. Assuming that fiscal policies are designed along the lines of social equity objectives, this would be the approximate cut-off level of consumption that may be considered as the basis for either granting welfare benefits or providing income tax exemption. In practice, the base consumption level cannot be determined; thus, the average consumption level of the society is used as a proxy.

The elasticity of marginal utility can take on any of a range of subjective values. If government is indifferent in terms of who benefits from additional consumption, then $\eta = 0$; this would give a distributional weight of 1 for each income group benefiting from the project. However, if government wishes to give more emphasis to consumption at lower income levels, η would take values greater than zero. Table 10A.1 shows the values that d may take as both η and the proportion of the base level of consumption in the consumption level of a specific group vary.

Savings Effect

To account for the savings effect, consumption is discounted in Equation 10.3 by a factor that is defined as the social value of public income (v). Conceptually, v is the welfare value of public income relative to the value of

Table 10A.1 Income Specific Distribution Weights

c_i	c^*/c_i	$\eta = 0$	$\eta = 1$	$\eta = 2$
$1,000	2.00	1.00	2.00	4.00
1,500	1.33	1.00	1.33	1.77
2,000	1.00	1.00	1.00	1.00
2,500	.80	1.00	.80	.64
3,000	.67	1.00	.67	.44
3,500	.57	1.00	.57	.32

Note. c_i is the consumption level of a specific income group i. c^*, used as a proxy for the base level of consumption, is the average consumption, and it is assumed to equal $2,000.

consumption at the margin. It is the ratio of a marginal increase in public income to a marginal increase in consumption. For example, when v equals 2.3, a marginal increase in income is 2.3 times as valuable as private consumption, the latter being expressed as a change in consumption of someone at the average level of consumption.

The use of this ratio is justified on the basis of the following premises: (a) Any increase in public income is likely to be used to upgrade social welfare through public spending on infrastructure or other productive public projects. (b) The present value of the net benefits that are expected to be generated from these ventures is likely to be valued differently by society than is present consumption when compared on the basis of a common numeraire. (c) Therefore, the welfare value of the public income generated by a project must be differentiated from the value of present consumption in accordance with society's preferences regarding the expected benefits from both forms of spending.

The formula used for calculating the social value of income is based on the following ratio:

$$v = \Delta W_g / \Delta W_c \, , \qquad (10A.5)$$

where ΔW_g is the change in the value of income and ΔW_c is the change in the value of consumption. To determine the value of v, the change in the value of income is converted into its consumption equivalent and expressed in terms of base-level consumption of the society, c^*. If the entire income or the return to one unit of investment is allocated to consumption, then Equation 10A.5 becomes

$$v = i/\rho \, . \qquad (10A.6)$$

The return to investment i in each period is discounted by ρ, which indicates society's preferences for present versus future consumption.

When only a portion of i is consumed, a residual that amounts to si accumulates in each period. This raises the capital stock by si, which in turn translates into additional consumption benefits. Assuming that s, i, and ρ are constant, we have

$$v = (1 - s)i/(\rho - si) \; . \qquad (10A.7)$$

Note that the proportion of marginal product saved, si, appears in the denominator. This makes sense because si accounts for the multiplicative effects of additional savings that are assumed to be reinvested.

Also note that this formulation does not allow for s, i, and ρ to vary. However, it can be used as an approximate estimate, assuming that these parameters remain constant over time.

NOTES

1. Another related argument is based on the view that government redistribution programs are likely to be more effective than a project's distributional adjustments. Subjective redistributions implemented at the project level will be quite marginal in comparison to aggregate measures that would redirect society toward its Pareto optimum-welfare maximum allocation. For more discussion, see Harberger (1971) and Tresch (1981, 543-5).

2. For a detailed discussion and description of alternative formulations of social welfare functions, see Johansson (1993, 15-21), Musgrave and Musgrave (1989, 73-84), and Stiglitz (1988, 102-11).

3. Point A cannot be attained in the second-best environment. Point D is Pareto efficient, whereas B is not, and B is the maximum attainable point given the market failures or public policy distortions characterizing the second-best economic environment. Of the two projects, the one that takes society to D has a higher present value because it moves the society to its first-best frontier. For more on the second-best analysis, see Tresch (1981, 51-9, 296-302, 544-5).

4. Notice that in this example, we referred to the Kaldor-Hicks criterion without considering the issue of the gainers compensating the losers. Realizing potential Pareto outcome, that is, requiring the losers to be compensated by the gainers, could also reduce welfare gains and result in rejection of an otherwise feasible project. For example, when gains and losses are weighted, the net welfare gain may be positive, but the gainers may be unable to compensate the losers when the unweighted net benefit is negative. For more on this, see Zerbe and Dively (1994, 236-53).

5. For more on distributional weights, see Feldstein (1974) and Gramlich (1990, chap. 7).

6. The derivation and the discussion of these parameters are provided in the appendix to this chapter. For more details on the World Bank methodology, see Squire and van der Tak (1975), Bruce (1976), and Ray (1984).

DISCUSSION QUESTIONS

1. Of the three alternative ways of treating the distribution question, which one is most in line with cost-benefit analysis?

2. Suppose the same project is reexamined under the three alternative ways of integrating the distributional aspects. Would the project show the same social benefit-cost ratios under the three approaches?

3. Is it possible for the free market economy to achieve an income distribution consistent with society's distributional norms?

4. Under what circumstances, do you think, does income distribution become an issue? Would you prefer the market solution over an approach that integrates distributional weights?

5. Compare and contrast the two different ways of deriving distributional weights. Which of the two sets would reflect society's distributional considerations more accurately?

6. What are the main limitations of Weisbrod's distributional weights? Despite these limitations, would you still consider this approach, or would you rather use the World Bank model?

7. Suppose the marginal propensity to save, $s = .3$, the rate of return to a unit of investment, $i = .15$, and the consumption rate of interest, $\rho = .07$. What is the value of the parameter v? What does it mean?

11

Applications of
Cost-Benefit Analysis

This chapter focuses on the real-world applications of cost-benefit analysis (CBA). As a foundation for the discussion of issues at the applied level, it begins by recapitulating some of the important conclusions from the preceding chapters. Analysts usually find a number of theoretical questions unresolved during the development stage of an evaluation problem. Is first-best analysis more appropriate than second-best? Should secondary effects be included in the overall evaluation? Under what circumstances should equity issues be raised? The answers to these and many other questions need to be clarified prior to the implementation of a cost-benefit study.

The chapter also provides a list of convenient rules to follow in a typical analysis. The list is not comprehensive, but it draws the reader's attention to those issues that have a significant impact on the outcome of project analysis. Finally, as an example of CBA design at the applied level, the chapter outlines the guidelines that the U.S. Environmental Protection Agency's Office of Pollution Prevention and Toxics (OPPT) uses for the evaluation of regulatory options.

ISSUES IN COST-BENEFIT ANALYSIS:
A RECAPITULATION

A keen understanding of welfare economics is necessary to conduct a complete and theoretically consistent project analysis. Highly sophisticated theorems and fairly complicated analyses aside, the ultimate goal is to select a project that will yield the highest possible social return. The CBA methodology is fairly straightforward, but the analytical details and the economic justification used at each stage of the analysis require experience with and expert knowledge of welfare economic theory. An analyst who lacks such training should at least have those theoretical issues that are critical to a cost-benefit study clarified before undertaking an evaluation task. Below is a summary response to some of the frequently raised questions in CBA.

Which economic and policy environment should be used in CBA?

Theoretically, CBA is developed for project analysis in a first-best policy and economic environment. Within the first-best framework, the public sector coexists with a competitive free market, and policymakers implement first-best measures in raising and appropriating the funds required for public projects: A lump sum tax is used to raise the public funds, and all needed appropriations for the projects are made in a nondistortionary fashion.

It should always be kept in mind that in real-world applications, first-best analysis serves as a theoretically convenient framework. It provides the necessary analytical details for the calculation of cost-benefit measures under ideal conditions and shows the extent to which such "theoretical" measures may differ from those obtained within the actual economic and policy environments. For a CBA analyst, the existing environment is second best, and as we have shown in the preceding chapters, projects must be evaluated and adjustments made in accordance with the second-best conditions.

Is CBA used to evaluate moves toward, on, or beyond the frontier?

CBA is a relevant analytical tool in an environment where public sector investments are intended to move the welfare frontier outward.

Movement toward or along the frontier is also possible and justifiable, as long as the welfare level improves and resource reallocation remains in compliance with potential Pareto optimality conditions.

Which of the benefit measures is relevant in CBA?

As discussed in detail in Chapter 5, the relevance of the consumer surplus notion depends on what purposes the concept is meant to serve. Benefit measures derived from compensated demand curves are appropriate and more accurate than the consumer surplus measure derived from the ordinary demand curve. Of the two compensated measures EV and CV, EV is superior in the sense that it provides consistent ranking when more than one policy alternative is under consideration. Neither measure, however, does well on practical grounds, and the choice between the two may be based on the nature of the particular policy environment.

For most analyses, given the difficulty involved in separating income and substitution effects, a statistical demand curve based on the Marshallian view of demand curves will suffice. If necessary, the analyst can also conduct a sensitivity analysis by estimating upper- and lower-bound surplus using CV and EV measures. Again, it should be emphasized that the notion of consumer surplus as developed in this text serves as a useful guide for the analyst to follow in identifying and measuring the net benefits of a project.

Should secondary benefits and costs be considered?

Secondary project effects should definitely be considered as long as they are nonpecuniary. All technical external costs and benefits should be carefully identified and measured. As emphasized in Chapter 5, environmental hazards such as increased noise and air pollution must be carefully identified and included in the evaluation as negative outcomes. Pecuniary effects, which are ordinary transfer payments, should be excluded from the evaluation. Such effects, although benefiting some, usually generate losses for others. They are also reflected in primary and secondary markets through the price mechanism or already considered when estimating the real direct effects. As a general rule, therefore, pecuniary effects must be excluded to avoid double counting. Note, however, as an exception to that rule that pecuniary effects may be taken into consideration when income distribution is at issue.[1]

Should the analyst rely on market prices or shadow prices?

Theoretically, shadow prices must be calculated if significant price distortions exist. When shadow pricing is incompatible with real-world applications, the analyst may rely on observed market prices. For example, despite the availability of information on the sources of price distortions, calculating shadow prices for marginal projects may be infeasible; it may be too costly to justify their use. When that is the case, the preferred practice is to point out the existing price distortions in the market and, through sensitivity analysis, ensure the accuracy of the evaluation.

For large-scale projects, the impact of unemployment in labor and capital markets should be reflected in the analysis, or, at a minimum, public policy makers should be warned of the likely impact of the unemployment conditions in factor and commodity markets on the outcome of the project. Sometimes, the price mechanism may account for distortions in factor markets. When there is unemployment, for example, wage rates are likely to be low, or at times of high demand for loanable funds, the rate of interest will reflect the intensity of the demand for the real value of the fund. This approach is fine as long as the price mechanism functions appropriately and real influences are reflected in prices with a reasonable time lag. Here, once again, the judgment of the analyst is important.

What is the appropriate discount rate?

This is not an issue in a first-best environment. The market rate of return reflects both the cost of capital and the private rate of time preference, and therefore, it is not necessary to calculate a shadow discount rate. There may be a need for adjustment, however, when there is a discrepancy between private and social time preferences. This may be the case if the analyst has reason to believe that the private rate undervalues public investment even in the first-best environment.

In second-best, real-world situations, it is difficult to make a case for or against any rate. Theoretically, the shadow price of capital approach is more accurate than the weighted average discount rate approach. However, it is a difficult approach to apply because shadow price estimates are very sensitive to the value of the marginal rate of return on private capital, consumer's rate of interest and propensity to save, the rate of reinvestment, and the treatment of the depreciation issue.[2]

The choice of a discount rate will also depend on the initial circumstances in the loanable funds market and the priorities given to consumption over savings. When such choices are difficult to make, applying a discount rate in reference to the standard pretax rate of return to private capital and the federal government's borrowing rates within a reasonable wide sensitivity testing range is advisable.

Is the income distribution question important?

In welfare economics, appraising a project in terms of its impact on society's income distribution is not the main concern. One possible explanation for overlooking the distributional aspects of public projects is that the question of income distribution does not lend itself to systematic treatment. Yet in the minds of public policymakers, income distribution is always important. The evaluation methodology may exclude the distributional weights, but in the final analysis, priorities and interest group pressures are likely to condition and influence the project outcome, which will probably favor one group over another. Therefore, it is always a preferred practice to provide as much information as possible on the impact of the project, including efficiency and distributional aspects. For a fairly complete project appraisal, social analysis that integrates distributional weights should always be provided with the economic analysis, even if the primary focus is on the economic efficiency question.

Which decision rule should be chosen?

In almost all analyses, the net present value rule seems to be the standard recommendation for project selection. However, the analyst should not rely on the net present value rule alone. Because the analyst's task is to facilitate the decision-making process, evaluation based on other criteria, such as benefit-cost ratios and internal rates of return, also should be reported so that the impact of the project can be assessed thoroughly.

GENERAL RULES FOR
IDENTIFYING COSTS AND BENEFITS

Having briefly clarified these frequently raised issues, we now provide six convenient rules to follow in a typical public project evaluation.

Define the Primary Real Output of the Proposed Project. The output can be any good or service, ranging from the functions of a public agency to increased scores in a local competency testing project. The best strategy in identifying project outcomes is to define the project's purpose clearly and identify the target population that it is designed to serve. Once the link between the purpose and the target population has been established, the primary output of a project becomes easily identifiable.

Do Not Use a Narrow Definition of Project Output. For example, the primary output of a project to increase the size of a police department can be identified as the number of cases that the officers may handle in a year; by assigning a social value to each case taken, the output may be expressed in dollar terms. This would be a narrow view of the project output. An alternative and more accurate approach would be to consider the marginal change in the crime rate within a defined region in a given year. As another example, the number of visitors to an amusement park built as part of revitalization and community development efforts may be too narrow a definition. Other measures reflecting changes in the overall economic activity in the community, such as changes in income per capita, new investments, and retail sales, would be more accurate.

Identify All Possible Outcomes Relevant to the Project. Use workable classifications and spreadsheets to distinguish between benefits and costs, real and pecuniary effects, and tangible and intangible outcomes. This is the most important stage in project evaluation. Even if some of these effects cannot be measured in dollar terms, they still need to be identified to show the impact areas of the project. This is an important rule to remember for almost every public project, but it is especially crucial in regulatory impact analysis because most regulatory initiatives have highly complex output and pricing implications in both regulated and unregulated industries.

Make a List of the Real External Effects. If a project produces external costs, such as air and noise pollution, carefully identify and list them as negative outcomes of a project. External benefits, if they exist, must be classified as positive outcomes. Avoid double counting by excluding pecuniary effects and financial transactions from the evaluation.

Exclude Transfer Payments. Specifically, taxes paid during the implementation of a project as well as subsidies given to promote and expand project outcomes must be left out of the analysis. Recall that real costs and benefits must be identified from the perspective of public interest. In this context, taxes and subsidies become mere transfer payments, and therefore they must be excluded to avoid double counting. Likewise, financial transactions, such as accounts receivable and payable, depreciation, and interest payments, must also be excluded. The rule to remember is to account for only those costs and benefits that relate to the actual use of resources as valued at the time they are employed.

Define the Boundaries of the Target Area and the Population for Which the Project Has Been Designed. At this stage, begin to articulate the analytical model and define the costs and benefits from the perspective of the population and the area to be served.

CBA DESIGN IN REAL-WORLD APPLICATIONS

Initiating and carrying out a cost-benefit analysis requires well-coordinated teamwork. Several support and functional studies, which generally provide the data needed to formulate the evaluation problem, need to be conducted before finalizing the design of the actual methodology. These studies include market surveys and analyses of demographics and regional characteristics, among others.

A critical examination of the circumstances surrounding the project and the justification for its implementation is usually a starting point. Viewing the perceived need for the project in the context of any of the market failures helps the analyst build an economic rationale for the project and thus conceptualize the general methodology to be followed in the evaluation. With the help of an extensive literature survey on the related topic, the analyst identifies those areas where data collection is needed and selects specific methodologies for the conceptualization and measurement of costs and benefits.

Literature surveys are very helpful, particularly in the case of transfer methods, where cost-benefit measures from related studies are adapted to the project under consideration.[3] This is especially useful when the contingent valuation method or any other direct or indirect benefit estimation method fails to produce reliable measures. If, on the other hand, the contingent valuation approach seems appropriate, then before undertaking the actual evaluation, it is often necessary to train a team of interviewers. This may require specific pilot case studies and practice surveys prior to the design and implementation of the actual survey.

Upon completion of these studies and other related preparation, the evaluation begins to focus on identifying, quantifying, and comparing the costs and benefits. Project selection (or project ranking, if there are several options within the project) is followed by the evaluation results, a sensitivity analysis testing of the results, an explanation of limitations of the evaluation, and a discussion of policy implications and recommendations.

As an example, a typical project evaluation design used by the OPPT is outlined below. Although the OPPT design may be unique to analyses considered under the Toxic Substances Control Act (TSCA), the steps involved in the identification, quantification, and selection process are applicable to the analyses of other types of regulatory actions.

Economic Analysis of Regulatory Options

The OPPT evaluation design consists of four sections: (a) definition of the problem and regulatory options, (b) benefits and costs of regulatory options, (c) cost-benefit results and sensitivity analysis, and (d) the impact of the proposed rules (U.S. Environmental Protection Agency 1993). The first section describes the problem and the purpose of the report, furnishes detailed information on the product proposed to be regulated, and provides an overview of substitute products, including existing regulations on them. The information provided in this section includes detailed summaries of the health and environmental risks stemming from use of the product and descriptions of the exposed population, including workers, consumers, the general population, and specific wildlife species. This section also discusses several regulatory options, ranging from labeling/information provisions to banning the product. Each option is carefully analyzed, and the economic rationale for its implementation is provided.

The second section defines costs and benefits and describes the methodology for estimating the net benefits of implementing regulatory options. The benefits category includes only reductions in risk to human health and environmental effects. All other resource effects that may be directly related to the regulatory option are included on the cost side.

Costs include (a) incremental costs incurred in compliance with the regulation, such as equipment, labor, raw materials, and so on; (b) administrative costs, including costs to the industries stemming from recording and reporting requirements; and (c) costs to the Environmental Protection Agency for implementation and monitoring. Using this fairly straightforward approach, cost data are collected and used to calculate the cost of each regulatory approach. Cost calculations are clearly explained, and the results are reported in present value or annualized terms.

Benefit analysis begins with risk assessment. Data on hazard and exposure are compiled to determine baseline exposure (expected level of exposure if the regulatory options are not adopted), which provides information on the exposed population and the level, duration, and frequency of exposure. This is followed by the calculation of the baseline number of cases for each category of exposed population, which, in the case of a ban option, will be the benefit of the proposed regulation. In a nonban situation, the expected postregulatory level of exposure, including the market effects of the regulation (reduction in the size of the exposed population because of an increase in the cost of the substance), is deducted from the baseline number to determine the number of cases avoided. Postregulatory risks of new exposure to substitutes, if they exist, are also deducted. Finally, the number of cases avoided is multiplied by the value per case avoided to determine the monetized benefits.

The monetized estimates are based on willingness to pay measures, which take into account direct medical costs, pain, suffering, foregone income, decreases in quality of life, and so on. The value of reduction in the risk of death is obtained from published research. Alternatively, direct evaluation methodology is used when willingness-to-pay estimates are unavailable.

In the third section, both benefits and costs are discounted to determine the net present value. The net present value is used as a recommended option, but when some of the costs and benefits cannot be expressed in monetary units, the analysis includes a discussion of such items. In this section, the report also provides a sensitivity analysis. Cost and benefit items that may be subject to uncertainty may be recalculated by using lower- and upper-bound values. If these estimates change the net present value of the project significantly, then alternative policies or more research to refine the data are proposed; otherwise, the ranking of the options remains the same.

Finally, as a supplement to the cost-benefit analysis, several studies are provided to examine the effects of the regulatory option in related areas. These include impact analyses to examine the effects of the regulation on small entities, paperwork burdens, trade, and equity.

SUMMARY

This chapter summarized some of the theoretical issues raised in the preceding chapters. The purpose of the summary was to recapitulate relevant generalizations and clarify issues that would guide the analyst through the application process of the CBA methodology. In addition to the list of rules to follow in a typical analysis, the chapter also outlined and described the essential steps of the evaluation guidelines used by the Office of Pollution Prevention and Toxics of the EPA.

NOTES

1. Also, as noted in Chapter 5, there are other exceptions to that rule: Secondary effects need to be considered when they represent repercussions for the profitability of the project and when losses cannot be recovered because they are nontransferable.

2. The treatment of depreciation and the rate of return to capital are particularly important because they affect the size of the calculated shadow price of capital.

3. For some examples of this methodology, see Desvousges et al. (1993), who use this method for the valuation of damage assessment, and Luken, Johnson, and Kibler (1992), who use it to value water quality impacts.

DISCUSSION QUESTIONS

1. What are the main theoretical issues that need to be clarified prior to the implementation of a cost-benefit analysis?

2. Determine if the following are true or false and explain why.

   Pecuniary effects, which are ordinary transfer payments, should be excluded from the cost-benefit calculations.

   One possible explanation for overlooking the distributional aspects of public projects is that, in the minds of public policy makers, income distribution is not important.

3. Under what circumstances will it be infeasible to derive shadow prices? What is the preferred practice when shadow pricing is incompatible with real-world applications?

4. What are the six rules to follow in a typical public project evaluation? Following these rules, identify the costs and benefits of a hypothetical project.

5. Using your example from the preceding question, make a list of the support and functional studies that may be necessary for your project design. Are these studies crucial for the completion of the evaluation? Discuss.

12

Evaluation Studies

Environment

This chapter and the one that follows review cost-benefit analysis (CBA) applications in two closely related areas: environment and health care. CBA studies in environmental economics revolve around the issue of negative externalities. Typically, the identification and measurement of costs and benefits associated with the internalization of an externality form the basis of the cost-benefit study. In the area of health care, however, the focus is on technical efficiency, and the perspective of the evaluation is usually the health care entity. Only a few recent attempts have focused on economic efficiency and used society's perspective in evaluating alternative medical procedures.

This chapter begins by highlighting some of the evaluation issues in environmental economics. An outline of the methods of benefit and cost assessment is followed by a case study featuring the main points of emphasis in the analysis of the costs and benefits of the Environmental Protection Agency's (EPA's) Great Lakes Water Quality Guidance. A review of evaluation issues and areas of CBA application in health care follows in the next chapter.

EVALUATION ISSUES IN ENVIRONMENT

As unintended outcomes, and with their effects working outside the price mechanism, externalities create increased health risks and environmental damage as both production and consumption activities from which they emanate increase. For example, respiratory illness is prevalent in regions where industrial air pollutants constitute the major source of poor air quality. Improving air quality standards in these areas will certainly reduce the occurrence of respiratory diseases.

A typical cost-benefit study of this or any pollution damage problem compares expected health benefits from improved air quality standards to the cost of designing and implementing pollution abatement programs. As illustrated in Figure 12.1, the MSB curve, representing the social marginal benefits from reduced pollution, shows that each additional level of pollution abatement corresponds to a lower level of marginal social benefit. This implies that the social gain from the first unit of pollution abatement is higher than that from the second unit. The MSC curve represents the social marginal cost of successive reductions in pollution. As the level of pollution abatement rises, the marginal social cost rises as well. The optimal level of pollution abatement is reached at the point where MSB crosses MSC.

To set standards at the optimal pollution abatement level and to achieve such standards, either by Pigouvian adjustments or marketable pollution permits, it is necessary to identify and quantify the marginal benefit of pollution abatement. This procedure is essentially the same for any externality problem: Benefit estimates are derived for an environmental policy or for a specific action aimed at preventing or mitigating the adverse effects of a pollutant. Although the procedure might seem quite straightforward, there are some complications. For example, factors other than air quality could lead to respiratory complications. Furthermore, because of the absence of the price mechanism, no direct measure of benefit from pollution control exists.

Methods of Benefit Assessment

There are several methods used in the literature to obtain benefit measures, either directly or indirectly. These include (a) the contingent valuation method, (b) the averting behavior approach, (c) the

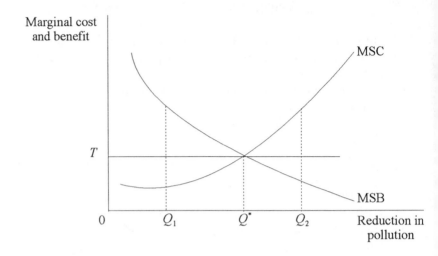

Figure 12.1. The optimal level of pollution abatement.

Note. Q^*, the point where MSB intersects MSC, represents the optimal level of pollution abatement. This level can be achieved by a corrective tax or a pollution permit. At Q_1, firms will be better off adopting a cleaner production process; at Q_2, they will be better off if they pay the tax or buy the permit.

travel cost approach, and (d) the hedonic price approach. As described in Chapter 7, the *contingent valuation method* relies on survey techniques to estimate the benefits of improving environmental quality. Survey techniques determine individuals' willingness to pay for an environmental improvement, or, alternatively, elicit individuals' willingness to accept compensation for deterioration of environmental quality. As a direct method, the contingent valuation approach is especially useful when there is no observable behavior that would avert the effects of pollutants.

The *technique of averting behavior* involves indirect benefit estimation from observed responses to a change in environmental quality. These include health responses to a pollutant and activities or products used as substitutes to avoid or mitigate the effects of a pollutant. For example, the cost of fume-catching canisters on cars or the cost of special nozzles on gasoline pumps can be used as proxy measures of the benefit from reduced fumes during refueling. This method establishes a linkage between pollutants and health response measures. But the extent of its use is usually controversial because of a lack of reliable data and the joint product problem.

The *hedonic price approach* decomposes the value of a resource, good, or service into the prices or values of its determinants. The value of real estate, for example, depends on the availability of public goods and services in the district where the property is located, including environmental amenities such as air and water quality. The marginal value of improved water quality is estimated from the hedonic price function by taking the partial derivative of the water quality variable. This approach is used in valuing environmental quality in urban areas and recreation sites and in estimating the value of life.

The *travel cost approach* links the total number and frequency of site visits to changes in environmental quality. It uses the travel cost to a specific site as a proxy measure of improved environmental quality. One problem with this approach is that there may be site attributes other than clean air and water quality that attract visitors.

All four methods have been used widely in the empirical analysis of nonmarket benefits. Recent surveys by Cropper and Oates (1992) and Smith (1993) provide an extensive review of this growing literature. Their findings include a variety of benefit estimates, ranging from statistical lives saved to the ecological benefits of pollution control. Some of the striking findings of these surveys include the following:

1. Studies on value of life provide a wide range of dollar estimates, with contingent valuation estimates exceeding the indirect estimates obtained from hedonic and averting behavior analyses.
2. Both the averting behavior method and the contingent valuation approach have been used for the valuation of morbidity, but neither method has provided convincing values.
3. Travel cost estimates of water quality differ significantly from the contingent valuation estimates, mainly because the former does not capture the nonuse values of water quality.
4. Contingent valuation studies of air pollution appear to be more precise than the hedonic property value studies; the latter method fails to decompose accurately the attributes of a house located in a nonpolluted area.
5. Contingent valuation method estimates of the ecological benefits of pollution control need to be used with caution; respondents to surveys

may be unfamiliar with or have limited understanding of animal and plant habitats.

Clearly, in spite of numerous advances in methodology in recent years, reliable estimates of environmental benefits remain elusive. Nevertheless, the indirect methods have established theoretically convincing linkages between nonmarket values and observed choices and thus have somewhat met policy-making needs. But as Smith (1993) cautions,

> Averting behavior, hedonic property value, and travel cost models measure what might be described as the privately "capturable" aspects of the environmental services being valued. Each method must "link" the nonmarket service to a private choice. To the extent that environmental services have public good aspects and that this "publicness" has value in addition to the private aspects, *none* of the available indirect methods will reflect these values. (p. 7)

As for the contingent valuation method, the main criticisms are that responses to elicited questions are hypothetical, that individuals may behave strategically in answering questions by over- or understating their willingness to pay for an improvement, and that individuals may be unfamiliar with the commodity and have no well-defined value for it. Therefore, individuals' responses may follow an inconsistent pattern (Viscusi 1990) and turn out to be unreliable or unsatisfactory (Cropper and Oates 1992, 710-1).

Also, when elements of risk are involved, the utility model to explain preferences may need to be modified to include behavioral factors. For example, Kunreuther and Easterling (1990) found no evidence that preferences for the proposed high-level nuclear waste repository at Yucca Mountain, Nevada, differed as the tax credit rebates offered to respondents varied at the levels of $1000, $3000, and $5000. The favorable response to the repository was entirely captured when the respondents were offered $1000, but higher levels of rebate did not gain support. Therefore, as Kunreuther and Easterling suggested, "some threshold level of safety" must be ensured before experimenting with this approach, and such safety may have to be supplemented by confidence-building measures.

An issue related to the valuation of environmental and health-related benefits is the discrepancy between empirical results and the theoretical justifications regarding the difference between WTP and WTA. As discussed in Chapter 5, for a welfare-improving change, the equivalent variation interpretation of WTA always exceeds the compensating variation interpretation of WTP. But it was also pointed out that the differences were minor and, as Willig (1976) demonstrated, they are likely to vary with the size of the income elasticity, a conclusion also confirmed by Randall and Stoll (1980) for the quantity change-related consumer surplus measure.

Reexamining the issue, Hanemann (1991) sheds further light on the discrepancy by showing that the difference between WTP and WTA mainly stems from the varying degrees of substitution between the public good and private goods. With the income effect held constant, the fewer substitutes available for a public good, the larger the differences between WTP and WTA. According to Hanemann, the empirical discrepancy is not a sign of failure of the contingent valuation method, but rather it is due to the lack of substitution between private and public goods. A recent work by Shogren et al. (1994) confirms Hanemann's conclusions. Based on the results of an experimental auction market design, the authors conclude that the divergence between WTP and WTA disappears for two private goods that are close substitutes but persists in the case of a nonmarket private good with imperfect substitutes, such as reduced health risk.

Boyce et al. (1992) also looked into the divergence problem, but from a different perspective. Moral responsibility of preserving an environmental good, if considered as a main intrinsic value attribute associated with such a good, may explain the disparity between WTA and WTP. For example, if individuals are asked to accept compensation to allow the extinction of endangered species, feeling the moral responsibility on their side, individuals will be likely to ask for large amounts; if, however, individuals are asked to pay to prevent extinction, they will feel morally less (or only partially) responsible and will be willing to pay less. As the authors conclude,

> A WTA measure of the value of preserving a species such as the blue whale clearly assigns moral responsibility to the individual. A WTP measure makes a much less clear assignment. That is, the framing effect caused by a difference in implicit property rights when shifting from WTP to WTA may contribute to the disparity between these measures. (p. 1371)

Cost Assessment

The preceding discussion focused on issues of benefit assessment with no attention given to the cost side of environmental projects. This is because most capital and noncapital costs of a project are directly measurable from the market, and when price distortions are present, adjustments are made to obtain the shadow prices. This is quite straightforward: Shadow prices for tangible costs are calculated using the techniques developed in Chapter 6; for the intangible costs and all likely damage assessments in areas where no pricing mechanism exists, the assessment methods described in the preceding section are used.

Also, there are cost effects that are usually difficult to detect. These include welfare losses in related segments of the economy that are due to price and output effects associated with pollution abatement measures. For example, the EPA's 1989 Regulatory Impact Analysis of controls on asbestos and asbestos products made several assumptions to operationalize cost data from complex intrasectoral linkages. The analysis assumed that no decline in prices of asbestos substitutes would be expected over time as market conditions for these substitutes change. It also disallowed cost-saving benefits that were due to lower-cost substitutes for asbestos-containing products. In the absence of asbestos-containing products, the analysis assumed a proportional increase in the existing market shares of nonasbestos products. Because of these assumptions, the Regulatory Impact Analysis provided overestimated cost figures, a limitation of the analysis clearly stated in the EPA report. It should be noted, however, that analysts usually account for such costs through sensitivity testing by setting upper and lower bound values.

COST-BENEFIT ANALYSIS
OF ENVIRONMENTAL PROJECTS

Failing to fully recognize the social component of costs and benefits of pollution abatement programs, private entities provide less than the optimal level of environmental protection. To offset this discrepancy, the EPA conducts cost-benefit analysis in areas where socially optimal abatement levels are needed. Benefit measures are expressed in monetary terms in very few of these analyses. During the 1981-1986 period, only five regulations (out of eighteen) involved cost-benefit comparisons (Cropper and Oates 1992). The majority of evaluations provide a detailed analysis of benefits but usually fall short of monetizing them. For example, the Regulatory Impact Analysis that was conducted in 1989 to identify and quantify the benefits and costs of various regulatory options for controlling exposure to asbestos fibers identifies only one source of benefits associated with reduced exposure to asbestos, and that is the reduced cancer cases. Other measures associated with reduced medical care expenses, increased productivity, and improvement in quality of life are not included. The analysis reports the number of cancer cases avoided because of the regulatory alternatives, and as a benefit-cost measure reports only the cost per cancer avoided. No attempt is made to monetize the benefit outcome.

The EPA study outlined below, on the other hand, weighs benefits against costs, and both are monetized. The monetized benefit estimates are based on applied research findings in environmental studies. This approach, known as the transfer methodology, is commonly used in the environmental literature to value damage assessment and environmental benefits.[1]

Costs and Benefits of the Proposed Great Lakes Water Quality Guidance: The Lower Fox River and Green Bay Case Study[2]

Developed under the Clean Water Act and the Critical Program Act of 1990, the Great Lakes Water Quality Guidance was proposed by the EPA for the protection of aquatic life, wildlife, and human health within the Great Lakes basin.[3] The Guidance provides direction on both water quality standards and antidegradation policies, along with methodologies and procedures for their implementation. The impact analysis conducted by the EPA provides a detailed examination of the costs and benefits associated with the Guidance: The benefit analysis is based on a case study approach, and the costs are estimated for the entire basin and the three case study areas.

The Lower Fox River and Green Bay is one of three case study sites used for the benefit analysis. Located in northeastern Wisconsin, the

Lower Fox River and Green Bay is a high-demand area providing access to a variety of recreational, commercial, and industrial uses. Recreational fishing and boating and facilities along the bay used for nonconsumptive activities, such as wildlife viewing and birdwatching, have been popular. The river has also provided process water for industrial use. However, the amount of commercial shipping has been declining, and some recreational activities, such as swimming and hunting, have been limited because of the river's increasing water quality problems and the loss of wetlands.

The source of these water quality problems has been surface water discharge emanating from forty-two industries and ten municipalities. Holding Wisconsin Pollutant Discharge Elimination System permits, these entities have been producing conventional pollutants and toxic substances, resulting in extensive damage in the area. Although the source discharges of the toxic substances have been declining over the years, they are still substantial and add to toxic contamination accumulated from past discharges.

Revised permit levels based on new water quality criteria will lead to changes in water treatment processes, and that will lower the discharges and loadings. The expected outcomes are changes in both water quality and the aquatic system, leading to improvements in fishery and other recreational activities. Attempting to quantify these benefits, the study provides a cost-benefit analysis comparing the quantified benefits to the costs of complying with the Guidance.

Benefits. The benefits were derived using one of two methods: (a) Benefit estimates of improved water quality are obtained, and a fraction of these benefits is attributed to the Guidance; (b) a benefit category is quantified at present water quality and increase in the value after compliance with the Guidance is estimated as the benefit of that category. Dollar values in both categories were based on applied research findings in related areas.

The study identifies a variety of toxic substances in municipal and industrial charges, including organic compounds, EPA priority pollutants, and resin and fatty acids. Estimating about a sixty-six percent reduction in pollutant loadings as a result of the Guidance, the study provides benefit estimates for a number of use and nonuse categories. These include recreational fishing, commercial fisheries, nonconsumptive recreation, and nonuse benefits. Other benefits, however, such as recreational boating and swimming, subsistence fishing, and waterfowl hunting, were not estimated because of a lack of data.

Estimates for recreational fishing were taken from applied research on fishery. The value for contaminant-free fishery (trout and salmon), ranging from $7.4 million to $26.2 million per year, was estimated using a travel cost method. The Green Bay area share of this value corresponds to between $2.2 and $7.8 million. Assuming that the Guidance contributes about fifty percent for moving from the baseline condition to the contaminant-free environment, the benefit attributable to the Guidance becomes $1.2 to $4.3 million in 1992 prices.

For yellow perch, another component of Green Bay fishery, an estimate of $1.8 million per year in 1992 prices is used. This represents the value for rehabilitating the fishery, which has been on the decline since 1965 because of overharvesting, pollution, and so on. Because it was difficult to predict the impact of the Guidance on yellow perch fishery, a wide range of 20 percent to 100 percent attribution was assumed, yielding a benefit figure of between $0.4 and $1.8 million annually.

The combined fishery benefits (trout/salmon and yellow perch) attributable to the Guidance thus amounts to between $1.6 and $6.1 million. Using an alternative approach from applied research on fishery, the report also estimates a value for the entire sport fishery benefits attributable to the Guidance of between $0.9 and $5.0 million. Based on the lower bound from the latter approach and the upper bound from the former approach, the report provides a benefit range of $0.9 to $6.1 million annually (Table 12.1).

As for commercial fishery, the impact of the Guidance is expected to be minimal. The sum of generated consumer and producer surplus, also based on the literature on fishery, is approximated to be in the range of $0.2 to $0.3 million per year.

The benefit estimate for wildlife observation is in the range of $1.3 to $1.8 million per year. This is based on the assumption that the Guidance may contribute to approximately a five percent increase in the baseline value of activities related to wildlife recreation. The baseline value, estimated in the range of $26.2 to $36.9 million, was calculated by multiplying 1.4 million activity days (an estimate from

Table 12.1 Summary of Annualized Benefit Estimates in 1992 Dollars (millions)

Category	
Recreational fishing	0.9 - 6.1
Commercial fisheries	0.2 - 0.3
Nonconsumptive	1.3 - 1.8
Nonuse/ecologic	0.5 - 3.7
Total	2.9 - 11.9

Source: RCG/Hagler, Bailly (1993, 8-26).

a local wildlife sanctuary at Bay Beach Park) by the value of each day, $18.71 and $26.34 (for these estimates, see RCG/Hagler, Bailly 1993).

Finally, the nonuse benefits (those benefits associated with a wide range of aquatic and wildlife species preservation) were estimated to be between $0.5 and $3.7 million per year. The lower bound estimate, $0.5 million, followed from the rule of thumb that approximates the nonuse value to be roughly fifty percent of recreational values. The upper bound estimate is based on willingness to pay for clean waters. Using estimates of willingness to pay from applied research findings in the environmental literature and the number of households within the study area, the report estimated a nonuse benefit value of $3.7 million per year.

Total benefits are shown in Table 12.2. The annualized benefit range is $2.9 to $11.9 million, with a midpoint of $7.3 million.

Costs. The cost estimates include fixed and variable costs incurred in adjusting the existing permit system to comply with the stated limits in the Guidance. They include capital costs, one-time special costs, and annual operating and maintenance costs. Estimated under four different scenarios, the total annualized costs range from $2.7 to $14.1 million, with a most likely cost of $5.1 million. The four scenarios were based on different assumptions regarding alternative permit limits, different pretreatment program costs, and different efforts of waste minimization costs. The most likely cost figure of $5.1 million is calculated under Scenario 2, as recommended by the EPA, and reflects the most stringent water quality-based effluent limits and the middle of the estimated range of waste minimization costs.

Table 12.2 Annualized and Discounted Benefits and Costs in 1992 Dollars (millions)

| | Benefits | | Costs | |
	Range	Midpoint	Range	Most likely scenario
Annualized	2.9 - 11.9	7.3	2.7 - 14.1	5.1
Discounted				
10-year phase-in	45.2 - 185.7	115.5	24.8 - 194.1	44.8
20-year phase-in	34.3 - 140.6	87.5	24.8 - 194.1	44.8

Source: RCG/Hagler, Bailly (1993, 8-28).

Table 12.2 provides both the annualized and present values of costs and benefits. The benefits are discounted at a three percent rate of social time preference, assuming that benefits phase in in ten years and twenty years. The costs are discounted at a seven percent interest rate, reflecting the opportunity cost of capital. Both costs and benefits are discounted over a thirty-year period.

It is clear from these figures that the cost of complying with the Guidance is somewhat in line with the expected benefits. However, the results depend on the attribution assumption made. The figures reflect an assumed attribution rate of fifty percent applied in the absence of data. A sensitivity testing conducted under alternative attribution assumptions resulted in costs exceeding benefits in larger magnitudes as the degree of attribution was reduced from twenty percent to one percent.

As the report concludes, the results of this study should be interpreted cautiously. Even though the study demonstrates the usefulness of CBA in evaluating environmental policies, several important questions remain at each stage of the analysis. Has the analysis identified all the relevant benefits and costs, or are there others to be considered? Have the analysts correctly anticipated the human response to changes in the environment? How relevant are estimates obtained in other regions to the conditions faced in this particular case? In the real world, an analyst can never be certain as to the correct response to these and other difficult questions. This is why CBA is often referred to as an art. Like any other criteria that may be used to evaluate environmental policy, CBA must be employed with proper respect for its limitations. However, when conducted properly, it can provide valuable information for decision makers.

SUMMARY

Having reviewed the four methods of benefit assessment (the contingent valuation, averting behavior, travel cost, and hedonic price approaches), this chapter concluded that all four have been used widely in the empirical analysis of nonmarket benefits. Despite possible complications stemming from insufficient data and the joint product problem, these methods establish theoretically convincing linkages between nonmarket values and observed choices and appear to meet policy-making needs.

The discrepancy between empirical results and theoretical justifications regarding the difference between WTP and WTA was also addressed. Attributing the discrepancy to variations in the size of the income elasticity, the discussion looked into the divergence problem from various perspectives.

Finally, a brief discussion of cost assessment of environmental projects was followed by the Lower Fox River and Green Bay case study. As the study shows, benefits associated with water quality are quite diverse, including both use and nonuse benefits related to aquatic life, wildlife, and human health. These benefits, based on applied research findings in the environmental studies, were estimated and compared to the costs involved in complying with water quality guidelines developed in accordance with the Clean Water Act.

NOTES

1. For reference on transfer methodology, see Chap. 11, n. 3.
2. Based on the final report prepared for the EPA by RCG/Hagler, Bailly, Inc. (1993).
3. The Guidance was published by the EPA in the Federal Register on April 16, 1993. Within the two-year period following publication, the Great Lakes states are required to have adopted water quality standards in accordance with the Guidance.

DISCUSSION QUESTIONS

1. Using real-world examples, describe each of the four methods of benefit assessment used in the environmental literature.
2. What are the main limitations of the method of direct benefit estimation?
3. In weighing benefits against costs, both need to be stated in monetary units. If a project's benefits are largely nonmarketed and cannot be obtained from observed responses to similar changes in environmental quality, then what approach do you think would be most appropriate to follow? Should the analyst dismiss the project? Use real-world examples in making your case.
4. Is the discrepancy between WTP and WTA significant? What may be the factors explaining the disparity? Under what circumstances do you think the difference will disappear? Use a real-world example to support your argument.
5. Outline the major benefit and cost categories of the Lower Fox River and Green Bay project. What method would you have recommended if the transfer methodology were not viewed appropriate to value nonmarketed benefits? For each category, justify your position.

13

Evaluation Studies

Health Care

Analysts in the area of health care have attempted to quantify health-related benefits, but because of the priorities of health care professionals and the uniqueness of the services provided in this sector, very few of these attempts have involved the cost-benefit analysis (CBA) methodology. There have been a few experiments to apply contingent valuation methods to estimate benefits in preventive health care, but these are still in their infancy. In addition to identification and quantification problems, ambiguities in the application of CBA concepts such as willingness to pay or accept, the choice of a discount rate in health care, and so on remain.

This chapter reviews some of the evaluation issues and applications of CBA in health care. A literature survey highlighting the application of CBA, cost-effectiveness analysis (CEA), and cost utility analysis (CUA) in health care is followed by two case studies that provide useful insight into how proposals involving HIV testing can be evaluated.

EVALUATION ISSUES IN HEALTH CARE

Traditionally, economists have concentrated on the issues of resource allocation and distribution, even in areas such as health care, where it has been difficult to define and quantify benefits. Yet studies using CBA in health care are quite rare. One possible reason for this is that the evaluation issues in which health care professionals are interested generally involve benefits that cannot be expressed in monetary terms. One other explanation might be that the analytical details required in a typical CBA demand familiarity with economic concepts and a foundation in welfare economics, and understandably, such preparation is often lacking among clinicians, who at this time seem to be under pressure to economize in their practices.[1]

There are also a few theoretical issues that need clarification. One interesting issue is whether the demand curve for medical care reflects the value that patients place on medical care spending. The traditional analysis takes the view that it does; individuals facing a price increase forgo treatments that they consider less valuable than their cost, and in this traditional framework, the treatment that individuals forgo is assumed to be the least effective one. But as the RAND Health Insurance Experiment shows, when faced with a price increase, patients tend to reduce all types of health care, including the high-valued ones. Such patient behavior contradicts the traditional demand analysis that, in response to a price increase, considers a change in the least valued care rather than all types; therefore, it is argued that the demand curve is likely to be a poor indicator of the value placed on health care services (Rice 1992).

Alternatively, evaluation of welfare changes could be based on medical effectiveness. But that raises the question of whether it is the patients or the experts who provide correct decisions regarding the value of a treatment (Peele 1993). According to Rice (1992), it is the expert who is likely to make the correct decision. But as Feldman and Dowd (1993) argue, "Measurement of consumer welfare should be based on the consumer's valuation of the advice, not the advice itself" (p. 199).

Although the issue of how to derive a willingness-to-pay methodology based on the expert's view is still under consideration, several studies have attempted to measure willingness to pay directly from patient responses (Johannesson et al. 1993) and indirectly from patients' relatives (Donaldson 1990). Employing a health production function, Johannesson et al. used a contingent valuation method to estimate willingness to pay by surveying 700 patients with high lipid levels. The survey included contingent valuation questions with yes/no answers to six response alternatives. Donaldson's UK-based study, on the other hand, relies on the responses of the relatives of residents in the National Health Services hospitals and nursing homes and looks into how much the government should pay for each type of care. This indirect approach, the author suggests, is appropriate for the evaluation of publicly provided health care programs.

Another controversy in the literature centers around the discount rate that should be applied to health care projects. A relatively high discount rate places more value on the well-being of the present generation over future generations. Of the two critical questions in this area, one involves the issue of discounting health benefits differently from the costs, and the other is to determine if the discount rate in health care should be different from the one used in financial markets (Olsen 1993). For both issues, the recent literature provides evidence consistent with the traditional view. Costs and benefits must be discounted by the same rate for consistency (Olsen 1993), and despite convincing arguments in favor of deriving rates exclusively for health care, research has yet to produce unquestionable support for such a position (Moore and Viscusi 1990). Preliminary research also has shown that individuals tend to place less value on lives saved in the future. For example, as Cropper, Aydede, and Portney (1992) have shown, "For a twenty-five-year horizon the future oriented program would have to save at least four times as many lives if it is to be preferred to a program that saves lives immediately" (p. 472).

CBA, CEA, and CUA in Health Care

As noted above, studies using CBA in health care are quite uncommon. There are a few studies that are labeled as CBA, but some are narrow in scope, focusing on technological efficiency rather than economic efficiency, and the perspective is usually the health care entity rather than society at large.[2] These include studies related to the efficiency of medical procedures, timing of treatments, alternative locations of treatments, and efficiency of treatments for different patient groups.[3] Even those studies that do use economic concepts defined from society's perspective tend to overlook benefits and costs that might accrue during different time periods and thus fail to derive meaningful benefit-cost ratios.

Because of the difficulties involved in identifying and quantifying health services, health care professionals use either CEA or CUA. As described in Chapter 4, CEA is often used in evaluating nominally unquantifiable output effects. Relying on technical efficiency as the main evaluation criterion and deriving a set of effectiveness ratios accordingly, CEA provides a yardstick for determining how effectively project goals are met. CUA employs an evaluation procedure similar to that used in CEA, but unlike CEA, it also considers the allocative efficiency criterion.

The project outcome in CEA is typically a single clinical outcome, such as years of life saved or an improvement in health status, and the goal of the analysis is to achieve maximum health effect at a given cost, or to achieve a clinical outcome at the lowest cost possible.[4] The analysis can be performed either for a specific treatment or for the purpose of ranking mutually exclusive or independent treatment programs. The evaluation of alternative procedures to treat a communicable disease, for example, falls under the mutually exclusive category. But the analysis of, say, three different communicable diseases will result in ranking independent procedures competing for budgetary appropriation. In either case, CEA is conducted with either a fixed or a variable budget.

The project outcome is defined differently in CUA. Instead of a single unit of clinical outcome, a health status index combining various health effects, such as quality-adjusted life-years (QALYs) or healthy year equivalents, is used. This version of cost-effectiveness study is especially useful in the case of ranking independent programs. As one step short of monetizing health care benefits, which is what is done in CBA, the derivation of a health status index makes cost-effectiveness comparisons among projects with heterogeneous health outcomes possible.

Because the health status index is utility based, CUA also considers allocative efficiency. However, in contrast to the economic efficiency notion used in CBA, the notion of allocative efficiency underlying

CUA is narrowly defined. It is based on individual perception, measuring QALYs and healthy years equivalent from the individual's perspective rather than society's. Society's perspective is employed only when externalities in health care are incorporated in the analysis. But when that proves to be difficult, as Labelle and Hurley (1992) argue, it may be more practical to reconsider CBA rather than integrate the externality issue in CUA.

Note that the majority of studies in health care do not distinguish between CEA and CUA.[5] They are treated the same, and in most studies, the effectiveness outcome is expressed specifically in either units or quality units. So, this distinction, or the lack of it, usually presents no concern as long as the study makes clear whether or not the outcome measure is utility based.

In closing this section, it should be pointed out that the majority of health care evaluation at this time involves CEA/CUA methodology with very few attempts at CBA. As indicated above, even those that are titled CBA fail to produce reliable benefit-cost ratios. However, as the number of studies employing direct and indirect benefit assessment methods in health care increases, the number of cost-benefit studies is likely to increase as well. Another prerequisite for genuine CBA in this area is increased familiarity with and a good grasp of economic analysis. Recent articles on health economics indicate that such awareness is on the rise and is likely to be a pathway to a burgeoning medical literature on CBA applications.

This chapter concludes with two case studies on the highly controversial issue of testing for human immunodeficiency virus (HIV). The studies on which we focus are recent, and even though they do not provide all the computations needed for a complete CBA, they do attempt to identify the costs and benefits of HIV-related programs in accordance with the CBA rules. The first study, conducted by Phillips et al. (1994), is in fact a cost-effectiveness analysis that provides estimates of monetized benefits as an extension of the study with no benefit-cost ratios attempted. The study by Holtgrave et al. (1993) is geared to standard CBA; benefits are carefully defined from society's perspective, but not all are incorporated into the cost-benefit computation. Overall, however, both studies provide useful insight into how a project involving this controversial issue can be evaluated.

Evaluation of HIV Testing: Two Case Studies

The study by Phillips et al. (1994) conducts CEA and CBA of alternative policies for HIV testing of health care workers (HCWs), including physicians, surgeons, and dentists. Policy options consist of mandatory and voluntary testing, and for those whose test outcome is HIV-positive, the options include mandatory exclusion from patient care, restriction of practice, and/or a requirement for the health care workers to inform the patients of their serostatus.

Analyzing all options under high, medium, and low HIV prevalence and transmission risk scenarios, the study concludes that one-time mandatory testing with mandatory restriction of practice is more cost effective than the other options. Under the mandatory restriction, the incremental cost per infection averted is estimated to be $291,000 for surgeons, including other physicians, and $500,000 for dentists. Note that the mandatory exclusion is, in fact, the lowest for both HCW categories, but deciding that this is not a viable option, the analysts focus on the mandatory testing with restriction of practice option.

The analysts also find the evaluation results highly sensitive to variations in prevalence and transmission risk. The incremental cost per infection averted ranges from $29.8 million (low prevalence/transmission risk) to a saving of $81,000 (high prevalence/transmission risk) for surgeons and from an incremental cost of $447 million to a saving of $57,000 for dentists.

The derivation of costs in this study is based on cost data obtained from extensive literature review and consultation with experts. These costs include three components: (a) counseling and testing costs, (b) additional treatment costs because of early detection of HIV-positive cases, and (c) medical care costs averted per patient infection averted. From these categories, costs are estimated by subtracting (c) from (a) + (b).

The authors also conducted a cost-benefit analysis by monetizing the value of patient cases averted and HCWs' lost productivity because of mandatory exclusion. Note that benefit-cost ratios or NPV in this study could have been calculated by willingness-to-pay estimates obtained from the literature on valuation of life. But because of "data uncertainty and differing approaches to valuation of life," the authors chose a threshold approach—a method to determine the dollar amount that the value of one patient infection averted must exceed for the mandatory testing to yield net benefits. Assuming that HCWs testing HIV-positive lose an average of seven years of income if excluded from practice, and half of that if restricted from performing invasive procedures, the authors estimated threshold values under different assumptions of HCWs' productivity losses. At zero productivity loss, this value was determined to be $271,000 for surgeons and $471,000 for dentists. They also estimated the value of $20 million (surgeons) and $13 million (dentists) in the case of restricted practice and $43 million (surgeons) and $28 million (dentists) in the case of exclusion from practice.

Note that because of insufficient data, several potential costs and benefits were not incorporated in the analysis. As the authors note, these include

> all the potential costs and benefits of testing programs, including some costs of program administration, the potential prevention of secondary HIV infections or other effects of testing, potential discrimination against HIV-positive HCWs and those who might be falsely identified as HIV-positive, and the value to patients of reduced risk of HIV infection from providers. (p. 857)

Therefore, the results should be used with caution. Refraining from making any recommendation for this highly sensitive issue, the authors conclude that

> our analysis neither justifies nor precludes a mandatory testing policy. Further research on the key data inputs is needed. Given the ethical, social, and public health implications, mandatory testing policies should not be implemented without greater certainty as to their cost-effectiveness. (p. 851)

The study by Holtgrave et al. (1993) compares the economic costs and benefits of publicly funded HIV counseling, testing, referral, and partner notification services (CTRPN). The U.S. Centers for Disease Control and Prevention (CDC) provides more than $100 million annually to states, cities, territories, and the District of Columbia for these services. The purpose of the evaluation is to determine if the program's benefits justify its costs.

Employing a societal perspective in identifying the costs and benefits, the study makes three assumptions: (a) CTRPN services will not be available without public funding, (b) 20 new HIV infections are averted for every 100 HIV-seropositive individuals reached by CTRPN services, and (c) the cost of alerting the population to HIV/AIDS issues and CTRPN services is assumed to be approximately sixty percent of program costs.

The cost component of the cost-benefit ratio (C) is estimated to be $188.2 million adjusted to 1990 dollars. This sum consists of $117.6 million for program costs and $70.6 for ancillary costs, including spending for HIV/AIDS surveillance, outreach, and national information campaigns.

The benefit estimate (B) is $3,781.9 million, and it is calculated by using the following formula:

$$B = LP \times E(TC + HC),$$

where LP is the number of individuals learned to be HIV-positive, E is the number of HIV-positive individuals who reduce risky behavior to the extent that they will prevent transmission of HIV infection to at least one other individual, TC is the lifetime treatment cost, and HC is the value of life based on a human capital approach.

For the base case scenario, E was estimated to be 36,505 individuals based on information obtained from the CDC's Client Record Database and published studies. The lifetime treatment costs, TCs, include costs incurred during the incubation period and beyond. Assuming an expected incubation period of ten years and approximately two years of expected survival with AIDS, the authors estimated discounted lifetime TCs of about $85,000 (ten years at $5,510 and two years at $42,500, discounted at six percent). The treatment cost of $5,510 during the incubation period and the treatment cost of $42,500 in the following two years were obtained from Hellinger (1991). Finally, the value of life, HC, taken from McKay and Phillips (1991), is adjusted to 1990 dollars. This estimate, discounted at six percent and set at $433,000, assumes the average patient with AIDS is thirty-seven years old at the time of diagnosis.

Using these base case estimates the study finds a high benefit-cost ratio of 20.09. The authors also conduct a sensitivity analysis by testing 0.2 and 1.0 ancillary cost fractions and twenty percent and fifty percent of prevented HIV infections. In all cases, the benefit-cost ratios were quite large. The benefit-cost ratios decline significantly in only one case; that is, when the possibility of increased unsafe behavior because of some individuals learning their HIV seronegativity status is allowed.

Overall, however, the study favors strongly the CTRPN services. The outcome of the analysis is even more favorable when certain limitations on the benefit side are considered. As noted by the authors, benefit estimates are conservative because of omission of benefits such as the positive impact of CTRPN on the blood supply, the possibility of delayed mortality because of early HIV treatment, and the possibility of reduced risk for those who are tested HIV-negative. In addition, the use of the willingness-to-pay method to place a value on human life would have produced higher benefits, thus yielding larger benefit-cost ratios.

SUMMARY

Some of the points highlighted in this chapter include the following: (a) Only a few recent attempts have focused on economic efficiency and used society's perspective in evaluating alternative medical procedures. (b) In most health care evaluations, the emphasis is on technological efficiency, and the perspective of the evaluation is the health care entity. (c) Because of the difficulties involved in identifying and quantifying health services, most analysts have used either CEA or CUA. (d) Cost-benefit studies are rare but expected to increase as the number of benefit assessment methods in health care increases.

The two case studies provided in the chapter focus on the issue of testing for AIDS. Both studies provide useful insight into how a project involving such a controversial issue can be evaluated using both CEA and CBA. Based on cost data obtained from extensive literature review and consultation with experts, the first study concludes that one-time mandatory testing with mandatory restriction of practice is more cost-effective than other options. The second study strongly favors HIV counseling, testing, referral, and partner notification services. Employing a societal perspective in identifying costs and benefits and using data based on the CDC's Client Record Database and published studies, the study finds a high benefit-cost ratio of 20.09.

NOTES

1. In view of the benefits to be gained from increasing the clinicians' familiarity with economic concepts, several articles have appeared in the medical literature explaining basic concepts in health economics and economic evaluation. See, for example, Drummond et al. (1987) and Eisenberg (1989).

2. In a survey of studies published in medical journals, for example, Udvarhelyi et al. (1992) reported that very few adhered to the basic principles and analytical techniques of CBA and CEA.

3. For a review of the CBA as well as the CEA literature, see Warner and Luce (1982, chap. 4) and Schofield (1987, chap. 16).

4. For a most recent comprehensive review of CEA of life-saving opportunities, for example, see Tengs et al. (1994).

5. For a discussion of the differences between CEA and CUA, see Birch and Gafni (1992).

DISCUSSION QUESTIONS

1. Outline the main evaluation issues reviewed in this chapter and, using real-world examples, show why each of these issues is important when it comes to evaluating health care projects.

2. What are the main reasons for not using CBA in health care as frequently as CEA and CUA?

3. How does CEA differ from CUA? Which method do you think is more appropriate for the evaluation of health care projects?

4. Explain the main differences and similarities between CUA and CBA.

5. Outline the main limitations of the two case studies included in the chapter and show how you might overcome these limitations.

14

CBA in a
Developing Country Context

The evaluation methodology discussed in previous chapters implicitly assumed that there were neither barriers to trade nor foreign exchange restrictions. Even when such assumptions were not explicitly stated, the quantity of traded goods relevant to public projects and the degree of trade distortions, if they did exist, were assumed to be fairly insignificant.

However, these generalizations are, for the most part, incompatible with the economic reality of developing countries, where the effects of a project on the country's foreign trade and exchange balances are quite substantial. Developing countries usually experience capital deficiency and foreign exchange bottleneck. This is one reason that most of the development projects initiated in such nations are aimed at generating or saving foreign currency. Investments in nontraded sectors, which depend on imported inputs, also have a significant effect on foreign exchange flows. When this is the case, the derivation of reliable measures for both traded and nontraded goods of a project becomes an issue.

This chapter focuses on project appraisal in a developing country context. The first two sections review the theory behind and the main features of the methodologies used to evaluate development projects.

The third section examines the current state of the art as practiced by private and international agencies, points out its limitations, and concludes with some observations regarding real-world applications.

THE UNDERLYING THEORY

The selection of a pricing methodology in CBA is a continuing concern among development economists. An observed market price, which reflects resource scarcities in a competitive market, is less precise when market imperfections prevail, leading to inappropriate choices of projects in distorted environments. The question arises as to whether it is sufficient to use observed market prices despite the real-world complexities, or if it is necessary to compute shadow prices in determining the social and economic value of competing projects.

The traditional approach to cost-benefit analysis is noncontroversial on this issue. Shadow prices must be derived and used whenever a market departs from its perfectly competitive setting. As clearly stated in the preceding chapters, cost-benefit measures are defined in a competitive economic environment and corrected for possible distortions following neoclassical optimization rules. To recapitulate some of these rules: (a) market prices are generated by a clearance mechanism that operates in a first-best policy environment, (b) individuals decide according to Paretian types of optimization functions and budget constraints, and (c) property rights are clearly defined and transaction costs are zero. Under these assumptions, market prices reflect both consumption values and production costs, and in equilibrium, they represent the marginal costs and benefits of society's output.

In economies where there are no barriers to foreign trade, the domestic price ratio and the world price ratio are equal. In addition to society remaining at the free trade equilibrium, it is also assumed that there are no market imperfections. As long as society stays at this first-best equilibrium, world prices remain identical to domestic prices, and both represent social costs and benefits.

A different result is reached in a second-best environment. When the price mechanism is noncompetitive (market prices deviate from production costs) and/or a tariff on imports moves society away from a free-trade position, domestic prices will no longer be equal to world prices. Other trade restrictions, such as quotas, taxes, and subsidies, also cause domestic prices to deviate from world prices.[1]

This divergence can be corrected by assigning domestic prices to nontraded goods and converting the world prices of the traded goods to their domestic price equivalents using shadow exchange rates. Alternatively, it can be corrected by using world prices for both traded and nontraded goods.

Both procedures are used in practice. The former approach, known as the United Nations Industrial Development Organization (UNIDO) approach, was developed by Dasgupta, Sen, and Marglin (1972). The latter procedure, known as the World Bank model, is well articulated by Squire and van der Tak (1975) as an adaptation of the Little and Mirrlees (1974) model.[2] Below is a brief review of the main aspects of both methods.

THE UNIDO GUIDELINES
AND THE WORLD BANK MODEL

The UNIDO model and the World Bank model are essentially the same. What distinguishes the two approaches is that the UNIDO model uses consumption as a numeraire, whereas the World Bank model uses uncommitted public income.

The UNIDO Guidelines

Under the UNIDO Guidelines, a project is evaluated in three stages: the calculation of financial profitability, the derivation of economic efficiency (shadow) prices, and the measurement of distributional impact.[3] Financial analysis is based on observed market prices. Using standard financial tools, such as the income statement, balance sheet, and cash flow tables, the analyst calculates the net financial benefit (NFB) for the project. This is followed in the second stage by the economic evaluation, by which NFB is transformed into net economic benefit (NEB) using adjustment factors. Finally, in the third stage, NEB, expressed in efficiency measures, is converted into net social benefit (NSB) using distribution adjustment factors. Thus, the analyst gradually moves from financial analysis to economic analysis and then to social analysis. Economic evaluation relies on the efficiency criterion, and social evaluation relies on both efficiency and equity criteria. Throughout the analysis, the UNIDO Guidelines use domestic prices as a numeraire. Nontraded goods are measured in domestic prices, and traded goods are converted into their domestic price equivalents by shadow prices. The basis of both economic and social evaluations is the project's impact on the national economy. When the impact is on consumption within the economy, the basis for shadow pricing is consumer willingness to pay; when the impact is on production, it is the production cost. And when the impact is on international trade, the shadow price is either the value of exports or the cost of imports.

The conversion of border prices into their domestic equivalents is done with the shadow exchange rate. The formula used for calculating the average shadow exchange rate is

$$SER = OER \left[\frac{(M_n + T_n) + (X_n + S_n)}{M_n + X_n} \right],$$
(14.1)

where *OER* is the official exchange rate; *M* is the cost, insurance, and freight value of imports; *X* is the free on board value of exports; and *T* and *S* are the import tax revenues and export subsidies for Year *n*. After converting the economic values of all traded inputs and outputs into their domestic price equivalents, the economic net present value is then calculated by using consumer rate of interest as the discount rate.

Finally, the project's impact on savings and investment is calculated to include both intertemporal and intratemporal income distribution effects in the evaluation. This is done by calculating distribution adjustment factors to convert economic efficiency values into social values. Assuming that savings are more valuable than consumption, especially in the case of scarcity of capital, the UNIDO Guidelines introduce a saving adjustment factor to convert savings into their equivalent consumption values, with a premium placed on savings induced by the project. Distribution adjustment factors are also calculated to reflect the premium attached to income groups below or above a base level of consumption.

Note that the procedure used by UNIDO to make the savings and distributional adjustments is essentially the same as the one used in the World Bank model. The difference between the two models is in the numeraire used: Whereas the UNIDO approach converts savings to consumption to make the distributional adjustment, the World Bank model discounts consumption to its savings equivalent. This is discussed in the following section.

The World Bank Model

The World Bank model consists of a set of rules to be used in measuring costs and benefits. Goods that belong to the traded category are measured in border prices; nontraded goods are valued at domestic prices and converted into their border price equivalents. The general form for these calculations is

$$P_i^* = \mathrm{cf}P_i \, , \tag{14.2}$$

where P_i^* is the shadow price, cf is the conversion factor, and P_i is the observed market price of commodity i expressed in domestic currency.

The standard conversion factor (α) and specific conversion factors for broad categories of nontraded goods (β_j) are calculated as follows:

$$cf = \frac{\sum m_i + \sum x_i}{\sum (m_i + t_i) + \sum (x_i + s_i)} \, , \tag{14.3}$$

where m_i and x_i are the values of imports and exports of i goods, and t_i and s_i are the import duty and export subsidy weights.

The standard conversion factor is obtained from aggregate trade data weighted by rates of import duties and export subsidies. It is used to shadow price traded goods for which world prices are not readily available or cannot be classified under any of the specific commodity categories. Conversion factors for broad categories, such as $ß_c$ for consumption goods and $ß_k$ for producer goods, are used for calculating shadow prices for the primary factors (such as labor, land, and capital) and the majority of nontraded inputs and outputs. Also, for nontraded inputs, such as utilities, transportation, and so on, conversion factors are calculated by a decomposition process that ultimately links the value of traded goods to that of nontraded goods.

To illustrate the use of conversion factors, let us use a simple example. Suppose an irrigation project is being considered in a region of a developing country where the main exportable crop is corn. The project requires initial capital costs of 20 million in domestic currency units (DCU) and is expected to generate an additional crop production of 2 million bushels annually. At a price of DCU 1.5 per bushel, the annual benefits of the project are expected to be DCU 3 million. Annual costs, consisting of wages and salaries, equipment replacement, and operation and maintenance, are expected to total DCU 650,000. The project's lifetime is assumed to be thirty years.

The annual net benefits of the project when measured in observed market prices amount to DCU 2,350,000 (3,000,000 − 650,000). To convert these figures into their border price equivalent, we use conversion factors. The conversion factors for this calculation are given as follows: $\alpha = .85$, $\beta_c = .87$, and $\beta_k = .84$.

The border price equivalent value of initial capital costs can be either directly measured in border prices or converted into their border price equivalent value by using the standard conversion factor. Using the conversion approach, we multiply DCU 20 million by the standard conversion factor .85 to estimate the border price equivalent value of DCU 17 million for the initial capital costs (Table 14.1).

The border price equivalent value of annual costs amounts to DCU 553,600, which is calculated as follows: Wages and salaries are multiplied by the consumption conversion factor (200,000 × .87), operations and maintenance are multiplied by the standard conversion factor (160,000 × .85), and equipment replacement cost is multiplied by the production conversion factor (290,000 × .84).

The value of annual output, also directly measured by border prices or converted into border prices by using the standard conversion factor, is calculated as DCU 2,550,000 (3,000,000 × .85). Thus, the annual net benefits of the project stated in border prices comes to DCU 1,996,400 (2,550,000 − 553,600).

Table 14.1 Initial Capital Costs and Projected Annual Costs and Benefits in
Domestic Currency Units (DCU)

	Market price	Conversion factor	Efficiency price
Capital costs	20,000,000	.85	17,000,000
Revenues	3,000,000	.85	2,550,000
Costs	650,000		553,600
Wages	200,000	.87	174,000
Equipment	290,000	.84	243,600
Operations	160,000	.85	136,000
Net benefits	2,350,000		1,996,400
NPV at eight percent, thirty years	6,455,830		5,471,071

The initial capital costs and net benefits expressed in border price
equivalent domestic currency units can be presented in the following
form:

Year	0	1	2	30
Benefits	—	1,996,400	1,996,400	1,996,400
Costs	17,000,000	—	—	—

Using a discount rate of eight percent (the marginal product of capital
converted into its border price equivalent by use of the standard
conversion factor), the net economic benefit of the project (NPV
measured in efficiency prices) comes to DCU 5,475,071 [17,000,000
− (1,996,400 × 11.2578)]. This figure reflects the economic efficiency
value of the project to society and is smaller than the financial figure
based on observed market prices.

Social Evaluation

The next step in project evaluation involves the conversion of the
net economic benefits (NEB) of a project into NSB. The net economic
benefits (costs and benefits measured in efficiency prices) consist of
savings (S) and consumption (C), and both categories can be stated
in terms of a welfare function:

$$NSB = NEB \times W, \qquad (14.4)$$

or

$$NSB = SW_s + CW_c, \qquad (14.5)$$

where W_s and W_c are the marginal increases in social welfare resulting from the marginal changes in savings and consumption, respectively.

Assuming that the marginal increases in social welfare because of marginal changes in public revenues (W_g) and savings (W_s) are equally valuable—that is, $W_s = W_g$—and that both can be expressed at the welfare value of base consumption level, Equation 14.5 can be stated as

$$NSB = S + C\,(W_c/W_g) \qquad (14.6)$$

or, using the standard notation,

$$NSB = S + C\,(d/v), \qquad (14.7)$$

where d stands for the social value of private consumption and v is the social value of savings. Note that when project benefits are measured in consumption, v is applied as a premium on savings. On the other hand, if public income is the unit of account, which is the approach taken by the World Bank model, then v is treated as the social value of public income and, as shown in Equation 14.7, is used for discounting private consumption.

To illustrate the use of both parameters, let us now convert the NEB of the irrigation project in the preceding example into NSB. Suppose the NEB of the project, which has passed the efficiency test, is broken into DCU 1,095,071 of savings and DCU 4,380,000 of consumption. Also, assume the weighted average of d is 3.5 and v is 3.27. Using Equation 14.7, the economic value of DCU 5,475,071 is converted into net social benefits:

$$NSB = 1,095,071 + 4,380,000(3.5/3.27)$$

$$= 1,095,071 + 4,380,000(1.07)$$

$$= 1,095,071 + 4,686,600$$

$$= 5,781,671.$$

Note that in this example, v is used for discounting consumption. If the intertemporal adjustment had been left out, that is, if v had equaled 1, then NSB would have been higher, reflecting only the income distribution effect.[4]

THE REAL-WORLD APPLICATIONS
OF THE WORLD PRICE METHODOLOGY

The Little and Mirrlees model and its World Bank version as developed by Squire and van der Tak (1975) have been used in a series of country studies conducted by the World Bank. In most studies, conversion factors for consumer goods, producer goods, and selected nontraded goods were calculated using aggregate data broken into broad sectors (Bruce 1976). Although historical trade data were typically used, in one case, computations were made with generated data on expected values of tax and subsidy rates (Squire, Little, and Durdağ 1979). Also, to correct for trade distortions, only tariffs and nominal subsidies were considered.[5] Factors that account for price distortions resulting from quotas and foreign exchange constraints were omitted. One study, however, accounted for nontariff distortions by introducing a premium rate in the denominator of the equation (Mashayekhi 1980), but it was found significant only within a wide sensitivity testing range.

Note that many of these country experiments were conducted prior to 1980. During the following decade, there was a dramatic decline in the use of the methodology because of factors both internal and external to the World Bank. Discussing the current practice of the methodology, particularly within the World Bank, Little and Mirrlees (1994) believe that

Social pricing, using distributional weights, has been abandoned.
No distinction is made between public and private income, or between the uses of income—whether saved or invested.

Sectoral conversion factors are rarely if ever calculated and used.

Shadow wage rates are not systematically used or estimated.

The values of non-traded goods are mostly converted to border values by a single standard conversion factor. To put this in another way, there is seldom if ever any attempt to estimate the actual foreign exchange consequences of using or producing particular nontraded goods. It is also equivalent to saying that the relative prices of nontraded goods are assumed to be undistorted (except perhaps that taxes may be subtracted). (p. 208)

According to Little and Mirrlees (1994), there are several reasons for declining interest in shadow pricing, or in CBA in general, within the World Bank. These include

1. The change in lending practices, such as switching from project lending to structural adjustment and nonproject loans that require no cost-benefit analysis;
2. The reorganization of the World Bank in the 1980s, which eliminated the Central Projects Department and resulted in fewer resources having been assigned to project evaluation;
3. The increased complications faced by the analyst because of new concerns in cost-benefit evaluation, such as quantifying and integrating poverty effects, impact on the environment, and so on;
4. The methodological defects, which may have been one of the main reasons that the method has experienced diminishing acceptability over the years.

Despite these observations, pointing out the prospective benefits from a fairly complete cost-benefit analysis, Little and Mirrlees (1994) conclude that

in aggregate, much of the investment in developing countries has had very low returns. This is evident in the low growth of many of these countries during the 1980s. Project appraisal is an essential part of the business of avoiding these mistakes in the future. Good project appraisal is done by people with their own incentives, within organizations that wittingly or not set these incentives. Both environments of project appraisal, the intellectual and the political-organizational, are keys to the quality of selection overall. This needs to be most seriously considered by those who manage and create these environments. (p. 224)

SUMMARY

This chapter reviewed the underlying model and described clearly how adjustments for price distortions are made in both the UNIDO and the World Bank methodologies. The UNIDO model uses domestic consumption as a numeraire and converts the border prices to their domestic price equivalents using the shadow exchange rate. The World Bank model, on the other hand, uses world prices as a numeraire and converts domestic prices to their border price equivalents by using conversion factors. Both methods also make adjustments on equity grounds. With only differences in numeraire, they make adjustments for the savings effect as well as for income distribution effects.

Estimating the efficiency prices, the World Bank model classifies cost-benefit measures into three broad categories: traded goods, primary factors, and nontraded goods. The costs and benefits that fall under the traded category are valued in world prices. Primary factors and nontraded goods are valued in domestic prices and converted into their world price equivalents.

In practice, this approach is viewed as necessary because it avoids the real-world complexities that would make efficiency price computation impossible. Prior to 1980, the economic efficiency pricing and social evaluation including income distribution effect and savings effect had been used in various country experiments. During the 1980s, however, the use of this model declined because of factors both internal and external to the World Bank.

NOTES

1. See Srinivasan and Bhagwati (1978), Bhagwati and Srinivasan (1981), and Blitzer, Dasgupta, and Stiglitz (1981) for a description and detailed analysis of the world price methodology.

2. For more on the World Bank methodology, see Ray (1984) and Little and Mirrlees (1994).

3. The details of the stages of evaluation can be found in the working guide prepared by Hansen (1978).

4. For simplicity, the conversion from economic evaluation into social evaluation in this example is made by adjusting the net present values. In fact, this transition should be made before the discounting; that is, the annual net benefits should be

adjusted first and then discounted by a social discount factor also reflecting the distributional adjustment. Also note that the irrigation project example in this chapter is designed to show how the conversion factors are used. The derivation of specific conversion factors and the decomposition process to derive conversions for specific nontraded goods are fairly detailed, and the reader should refer to the original World Bank country studies. For more on conversion factors and examples of various country applications, see Bruce (1976), Squire, Little, and Durdağ (1979), and Mashayekhi (1980).

5. Coefficients taken from a country's input-output table also can be used as weights for the rates of import duties and export subsidies (Schohl 1979). This approach is based on the view that input-output coefficients track the entire effect of price distortions on the nontraded sectors and thus provide a fairly accurate estimate of domestic price variations.

DISCUSSION QUESTIONS

1. Can the standard project evaluation method developed in the preceding chapter be used in evaluating projects in developing countries? What might be the main complications if project managers in developing countries choose to do so?

2. Outline the main evaluation steps of the UNIDO Guidelines. How different is the methodology of the Guidelines from that of the World Bank?

3. Describe the method used in deriving the standard conversion factor. How does this factor differ from the other conversion factors computed for broad categories of nontraded goods? For what project-related commodity categories is the standard conversion factor used?

4. What does the social value of savings measure? Suppose this parameter is calculated as 3.25. What does this figure indicate when public income is used as a numeraire?

5. Suppose the net benefit of a project that has passed the efficiency test is broken into $400 of savings and $600 of consumption. Also assume the weighted average of d is 3.5 and v is 3.27. What is the net social benefit of this project? If the intertemporal adjustment had been left out, that is, if v had equaled 1, then what would have been the value of the net social benefits?

6. Outline and discuss some of the main reasons for declining interest in CBA in general within the World Bank. Should more weight be given to CBA in appraising development projects? Discuss.

References

Arrow, K. J., and R. C. Lind. 1970. Uncertainty and the evaluation of public investment decisions. *American Economic Review* 60:364-78.

Bator, F. M. 1957. The simple analytics of welfare maximization. *American Economic Review* 47:22-59.

Bhagwati, J. N., and T. N. Srinivasan. 1981. The evaluation of projects at world prices under trade distortions: Quantitative restrictions, monopoly power in trade and nontraded goods. *International Economic Review* 22:385-99.

Birch, S., and A. Gafni. 1992. Cost effectiveness/utility analyses: Do current decision rules lead us to where we want to be? *Journal of Health Economics* 11:279-96.

Bishop, R. C., and M. P. Welsh. 1992. Existence values in benefit-cost analysis and damage assessment. *Land Economics* 68:405-17.

Black, D. 1948. On the rationale of group decision making. *Journal of Political Economy* 56:23-34.

Blitzer, C., P. Dasgupta, and J. Stiglitz. 1981. Project appraisal and foreign exchange constraints. *Economic Journal* 91:58-74.

Boadway, R. W., and D. E. Wildasin. 1984. *Public sector economics.* 2d ed. Boston: Little, Brown.

Boyce, R. B., T. C. Brown, G. H. McClelland, G. L. Peterson, and W. Schulze. 1992. An experimental examination of intrinsic values as a source of the WTA-WTP disparity. *American Economic Review* 82:1366-73.

Boyle, K., and R. C. Bishop. 1987. Valuing wildlife in benefit cost analyses: A case study involving endangered species. *Water Resources Research* 23:943-50.

Boyle, K. J., W. H. Desvousges, F. R. Johnson, R. W. Dunford, and S. P. Hudson. 1994. An investigation of part-whole biases in contingent-valuation studies. *Journal of Environmental Economics and Management* 27:64-83.

Bradford, D. F. 1975. Constraints on government investment opportunities and the choice of discount rate. *American Economic Review* 65:887-99.

Broome, J. 1978. Trying to value a life. *Journal of Public Economics* 9:91-100.

Bruce, C. 1976. Social cost-benefit analysis: A guide for country and project economists to the derivation and application of economic and social accounting prices. World Bank Staff Working Paper No. 239. Washington, DC: IBRD.

Buchanan, J. M., and G. Tullock. 1965. *The calculus of consent.* Ann Arbor: University of Michigan Press.

Campen, J. T. 1986. *Benefit, cost, and beyond.* Cambridge, MA: Ballinger.

Coase, R. H. 1960. The problem of social cost. *Journal of Law and Economics* 3:1-44.

Cropper, M. L., S. K. Aydede, and P. R. Portney. 1992. Rates of time preference for saving lives. *American Economic Review Proceedings* 82:469-72.

Cropper, M. L., and W. E. Oates. 1992. Environmental economics: A survey. *Journal of Economic Literature* 30:675-740.

Cummings, R. G., D. S. Brookshire, and W. D. Schulze. 1986. *Valuing environmental goods: An assessment of the contingent valuation method.* Totowa, NJ: Rowman and Allanheld.

Cummings, R. G., L. A. Cox, and A. M. Freeman. 1986. General methods for benefits assessment. In *Benefit assessment: The state of the art,* ed. J. D. Bentkover, V. T. Covello, and J. Mumpower, 161-91. Dordrecht: Reidel.

Cummings, R. G., G. W. Harrison, and E. E. Rutström. 1995. Homegrown values and hypothetical surveys: Is the dichotomous-choice approach incentive-compatible? *American Economic Review* 85:260-6.

Dasgupta, P., A. Sen, and S. Marglin. 1972. *Guidelines for project evaluation.* New York: United Nations Publications.

Desvousges, W. H., R. W. Dunford, K. E. Mathews, and H. S. Banzhaf. 1993. NRDA case study: The Arthur Kill oil spill. Paper presented at the 1993 International Oil Spill Conference, March 29-April 1, Tampa, FL.

Desvousges, W. H., V. K. Smith, and A. Fisher. 1987. Option price estimates for water quality improvements: A contingent valuation study for the Monongahela River. *Journal for Environmental Economics and Management* 14:248-67.

Diamond, P. A., and J. A. Hausman. 1994. Contingent valuation: Is some number better than no number? *Journal of Economic Perspectives* 8:45-64.

Donaldson, C. 1990. Willingness to pay for publicly-provided goods: A possible measure of benefit? *Journal of Health Economics* 9:103-18.

Drèze, J., and N. Stern. 1990. Policy reform, shadow prices, and market prices. *Journal of Public Economics* 42:1-45.

Drummond, M., G. Stoddart, R. Labelle, and R. Cushman. 1987. Health economics: An introduction for clinicians. *Annals of Internal Medicine* 107:88-92.

Eisenberg, J. M. 1989. Clinical economics: A guide to the economic analysis of clinical practices. *Journal of American Medical Association* 262:2879-86.

Feldman, R., and B. Dowd. 1993. What does the demand curve for medical care measure? *Journal of Health Economics* 12:193-200.

Feldstein, M. S. 1964. The social time preference discount rate in cost-benefit analysis. *Economic Journal* 74:360-79.

———. 1974. Distributional preferences in public expenditure analysis. In *Redistribution through public choice,* ed. H. M. Hochman and G. E. Peterson, 136-61. New York: Columbia University Press.

Freeman, A. M. 1993. *The measurement of environmental and resource values: Theory and methods.* Washington, DC: Resources for the Future.

Gramlich, E. M. 1990. *A guide to benefit-cost analysis.* 2d ed. Englewood Cliffs, NJ: Prentice Hall.

Griffin, R. C. 1995. Economic efficiency in policy analysis. *Land Economics* 71:1-15.

Guess, G. M., and P. G. Farnham. 1989. *Cases in public policy analysis.* New York: Longman.

Hanemann, W. M. 1991. Willingness to pay and willingness to accept: How much can they differ? *American Economic Review* 81:635-47.

———. 1994. Valuing the environment through contingent valuation. *Journal of Economic Perspectives* 8:19-43.

Hanley, N., and C. L. Spash. 1993. *Cost-benefit analysis.* Brookfield, VT: Elgar.

Hansen, J. R. 1978. *Guide to practical project appraisal: Social benefit-cost analysis in developing countries.* New York: United Nations Publications.

Harberger, A. C. 1971. Three basic postulates for applied welfare economics: An interpretive essay. *Journal of Economic Literature* 9:785-97.

———. 1972. The opportunity cost of public investment financed by borrowing. In *Cost-benefit analysis,* ed. R. Layard, 303-10. New York: Penguin.

Harrison, A. J., and D. A. Quarmby. 1972. The value of time. In *Cost-benefit analysis,* ed. R. Layard, 173-208. New York: Penguin.

Hartman, R. W. 1990. One thousand points of light seeking a number: A case study of CBO's search for a discount rate policy. *Journal of Environmental Economics and Management* 18:S3-S7.

Hellinger, F. J. 1991. Forecasting the medical care costs of the HIV epidemic: 1991-1994. *Inquiry* 28:213-25.

Holtgrave, D. R., R. O. Valdiserri, A. R. Gerber, and A. R. Hinman. 1993. Human immunodeficiency virus counseling, testing, referral, and partner notification services: A cost-benefit analysis. *Archives of Internal Medicine* 153:1225-30.

Johannesson, M., P-O. Johansson, B. Kriström, L. Borgquist, and B. Jönsson. 1993. Willingness to pay for lipid lowering: A health production function approach. *Applied Economics* 25:1023-31.

Johansson, P-O. 1993. *Cost-benefit analysis of environmental change.* Cambridge, UK: Cambridge University Press.

Jones-Lee, M. W. 1994. Safety and the saving of life: The economics of safety and physical risk. In *Cost-benefit analysis,* ed. R. Layard and S. Glaister, 290-318. Cambridge, UK: Cambridge University Press.

Krahn, M., and A. Gafni. 1993. Discounting in the economic evaluation of health care interventions. *Medical Care* 31:403-18.

Kunreuther, H., and D. Easterling. 1990. Are risk-benefit tradeoffs possible in siting hazardous facilities? *American Economic Review Proceedings* 80:252-6.

Labelle, R. J., and J. E. Hurley. 1992. Implications of basing health-care resource allocations on cost-utility analysis in the presence of externalities. *Journal of Health Economics* 11:259-77.

Layard, R. 1972. Introduction. In *Cost-benefit analysis,* ed. R. Layard, 9-70. New York: Penguin.

Layard, R., and S. Glaister, eds. 1994. *Cost-benefit analysis.* 2d ed. Cambridge, UK: Cambridge University Press.

Levin, J., and B. Nalebuff. 1995. An introduction to vote-counting schemes. *Journal of Economic Perspectives* 9:3-26.

Lind, R. C. 1982. *Discounting for time and risk in energy policy.* Washington, DC: Resources For the Future.

———. 1990. Reassessing the government's discount rate policy in light of new theory and data in a world economy with a high degree of capital mobility. *Journal of Environmental Economics and Management* 18:S8-S28.

Little, I. M. D., and J. A. Mirrlees. 1974. *Project appraisal and planning for developing countries.* London: Heinemann.

————. 1994. The costs and benefits of analysis: Project appraisal and planning twenty years on. In *Cost-benefit analysis.* 2d ed., ed. R. Layard and S. Glaister, 199-231. New York: Cambridge University Press.

Luken, R. A., F. R. Johnson, and V. Kibler. 1992. Benefits and costs of pulp and paper effluent controls under the Clean Water Act. *Water Resources Research* 28:665-74.

Lyon, R. M. 1990. Federal discount rate policy, the shadow price of capital, and challenges for reforms. *Journal of Environmental Economics and Management* 18:S29-S50.

Marglin, S. A. 1963. The opportunity costs of public investment. *Quarterly Journal of Economics* 77:274-89.

Marshall, A. 1920. *Principles of economics.* 8th ed. London: Macmillan.

Mashayekhi, A. 1980. Shadow prices for project appraisal in Turkey. World Bank Staff Working Paper No. 392.

McKay, N. L., and K. M. Phillips. 1991. An economic evaluation of mandatory premarital testing for HIV. *Inquiry* 28:236-48.

McKean, R. N. 1958. *Efficiency in government through system analysis.* New York: John Wiley.

————. 1968. The use of shadow prices. In *Problems in public expenditure analysis*, ed. S. B. Chase, 33-77. Washington, DC: Brookings Institution.

McKenna, C. K. 1980. *Quantitative methods for public decision making.* New York: McGraw-Hill.

Mendelsohn, R. 1981. The choice of discount rates for public projects. *American Economic Review* 71:239-41.

Mishan, E. J. 1971. Evaluation of life and limb: A theoretical approach. *Journal of Political Economy* 79:687-705.

————. 1988. *Cost-benefit analysis.* 4th ed. London: Unwin Hyman.

Mitchell, R. C., and R. T. Carson. 1989. *Using surveys to value public goods: The contingent valuation method.* Baltimore: Resources for the Future.

Moore, M. J., and W. K. Viscusi. 1990. Discounting environmental health risks: New evidence and policy implications. *Journal of Environmental Economics and Management* 18:S51-S62.

Mueller, D. 1976. Public choice: A survey. *Journal of Economic Literature* 14:395-433.

Musgrave, R. A., and P. B. Musgrave. 1989. *Public finance in theory and practice.* 5th ed. New York: McGraw-Hill.

MVA Consultancy, Institute for Transport Studies at Leeds University, and Transport Studies Unit at Oxford University. 1994. Time savings. In *Cost-benefit analysis*, ed. R. Layard and S. Glaister, 235-271. Cambridge, UK: Cambridge University Press.

Nelson, J. R. 1968. The value of travel time. In *Problems in public expenditure analysis*, ed. S. B. Chase, 78-126. Washington, DC: Brookings Institution.

Nelson, R. H. 1987. The economics profession and the making of public policy. *Journal of Economic Literature* 25:49-91.

Ng, Y-K. 1979. *Welfare economics.* London: Macmillan.

Olsen, J. A. 1993. On what basis should health be discounted? *Journal of Health Economics* 12:39-53.

Peele, P. B. 1993. Evaluating welfare losses in the health care market. *Journal of Health Economics* 12:205-8.

Phillips, K. A., R. A. Lowe, J. G. Kahn, P. Lurie, A. L. Avins, and D. Ciccarone. 1994. The cost-effectiveness of HIV testing of physicians and dentists in the United States. *Journal of the American Medical Association* 271:851-8.

Portney, P. R. 1994. The contingent valuation debate: Why economists should care. *Journal of Economic Perspectives* 8:3-17.

Prest, A. R., and R. Turvey. 1965. Cost-benefit analysis: a survey. *Economic Journal* 75:683-735.

Randall, A., and J. R. Stoll. 1980. Consumer's surplus in commodity space. *American Economic Review* 70:449-55.

Ray, A. 1984. *Cost-benefit analysis: Issues and methodologies.* Baltimore: Johns Hopkins University Press.

RCG/Hagler, Bailly. 1993. Regulatory impact analysis of the proposed Great Lake Quality Guidance. Report prepared for the U.S. Environmental Protection Agency (April 15). Boulder, CO: RCG/Hagler, Bailly.

Rice, T. 1992. An alternative framework for evaluating welfare losses in the health care market. *Journal of Health Economics* 11:85-92.

Robinson, C. J. 1990. Philosophical origins of the social rate of discount in cost-benefit analysis. *The Milbank Quarterly* 68:245-65.

Rosen, H. S. 1995. *Public finance.* 4th ed. Chicago: Irwin.

Ross, S. A., R. W. Westerfield, and B. D. Jordan. 1993. *Fundamentals of corporate finance.* 2d ed. Homewood, IL: Irwin.

Schelling, T. C. 1968. The life you save may be your own. In *Problems in public sector expenditure analysis,* ed. S. B. Chase, 127-76. Washington, DC: Brookings Institution.

Schkade, D. A., and J. W. Payne. 1994. How people respond to contingent valuation questions: A verbal protocol analysis of willingness to pay for an environmental regulation. *Journal of Environmental Economics and Management* 26:88-109.

Schofield, J. A. 1987. *Cost-benefit analysis in urban and regional planning.* London: Allen & Unwin.

Schohl, W. W. 1979. Estimating shadow prices for Colombia in an input-output table framework. World Bank Staff Working Paper No. 357.

Sen, A. K. 1982. Approaches to the choice of discount rate for social benefit-cost analysis. In *Discounting for time and risk in energy policy,* ed. R. C. Lind, 325-53. Washington, DC: Resources for the Future.

———. 1985. Social choice and justice: A review article. *Journal of Economic Literature* 23:1764-76.

Shogren, J. F., S. Y. Shin, D. J. Hayes, and J. B. Kliebenstein. 1994. Resolving differences in willingness to pay and willingness to accept. *American Economic Review* 84:255-70.

Smith, V. K. 1986. A conceptual overview of the foundations of benefit-cost analysis. In *Benefit assessment: The state of the art,* ed. J. D. Bentkover, V. T. Covello, and J. Mumpower, 13-34. Dordrecht: Reidel.

———. 1993. Nonmarket valuation of environmental resources: An interpretive appraisal. *Land Economics* 69:1-26.

Squire, L., I. M. D. Little, and M. Durdağ. 1979. Application of shadow pricing to country economic analysis with an illustration from Pakistan. World Bank Staff Working Paper No. 330.

Squire, L., and H. G. van der Tak. 1975. *Economic analysis of projects.* Baltimore: Johns Hopkins University Press.

Srinivasan, T. N., and J. N. Bhagwati. 1978. Shadow prices for project selection in the presence of distortions: Effective rates of protection and domestic resource costs. *Journal of Political Economy* 86:97-116.

Stiglitz, J. E. 1988. *Economics of the public sector.* 2d ed. New York: Norton.

Stokey, E., and R. Zeckhauser. 1978. *A primer for policy analysis.* New York: Norton.

Tengs, T. O., M. E. Adams, J. S. Pliskin, D. G. Safran, J. E. Siegel, M. C. Weinstein, and J. D. Graham. 1994. *Five-hundred life-saving interventions and their cost-effectiveness.* Boston: Harvard Center for Risk Analysis.

Tresch, R. W. 1981. *Public finance: A normative theory.* Plano, TX: Business Publications.

Tuckman, H. P., and T. F. Nas. 1980. Measuring the effectiveness of instructional radio: The methodological issues. In *Economics of new educational media II,* UNESCO, 67-86. Paris: UNESCO.

Udvarhelyi, I. S., G. A. Colditz, A. Rai, and A. M. Epstein. 1992. Cost-effectiveness and cost-benefit analyses in the medical literature: Are the methods being used correctly? *Annals of Internal Medicine* 116:238-44.

U.S. Environmental Protection Agency. 1993, January. *Guidance on the preparation of economic analysis.* Washington, DC: U.S. Environmental Protection Agency.

U.S. General Accounting Office. 1992. *Discount rate policy.* GAO/OCE-17.1.1 (May). Washington, DC: GAO.

U.S. Office of Management and Budget. 1992. *Circular No. A-94 rev.* (October 29). Washington, DC: OMB.

———. 1994. *Circular No. A-94 rev., Appendix C* (February 10). Washington, DC: OMB.

Varian, H. R. 1992. *Microeconomic analysis.* 3d ed. New York: Norton.

Viscusi, W. K. 1990. Sources of inconsistency in societal responses to health risks. *American Economic Review Proceedings* 80:257-61.

Warner, K. E., and B. R. Luce. 1982. *Cost-benefit and cost-effectiveness analysis in health care: Principles, practice, and potential.* Ann Arbor, MI: Health Administration Press.

Weisbrod, B. A. 1968a. Concepts of costs and benefits. In *Problems in public expenditure analysis,* ed. S. M. Chase, 257-62. Washington, DC: The Brookings Institution.

———. 1968b. Income redistribution effects and benefit-cost analysis. In *Problems in public expenditure analysis,* ed. S. B. Chase, 177-222. Washington, DC: The Brookings Institution.

Weitzman, M. L. 1994. On the "environmental" discount rate. *Journal of Environmental Economics and Management* 26:200-9.

Willig, R. D. 1976. Consumer's surplus without apology. *American Economic Review* 66:589-97.

Zerbe, R. O., and D. D. Dively. 1994. *Benefit-cost analysis in theory and practice.* New York: HarperCollins.

Index

About the Author

Tevfik F. Nas is Professor in the Economics Department and the Master of Public Administration Program at the University of Michigan, Flint. His recent contributions include two edited books, *Liberalization and the Turkish Economy* and *Economics and Politics of Turkish Liberalization*, and a number of articles on macroeconomic and public policy issues published in various journals, including the *American Political Science Review*.